PRAISE

MOBBING: Emotional Abuse

With alarming detail and convincing data, readers learn how the horror of events common to school yards occur daily, at every level of the hierarchy, in adult work organizations, sapping individual initiative, productivity, and well-being. MOBBING is a book for anyone who has ever been a target of a group's violence and for those who have responsibility for stopping it. In other words, it is a book for us all.

—Harvey A. Hornstein, Ph.D.,
Columbia University, Department of Organization & Leadership
and Author of *Brutal Bosses and Their Prey*

I highly recommend MOBBING to managers and employees alike. I have seen employees mobbed by managers and the system, and I have seen managers mobbed by their employees. Until recently, the syndrome did not have a name. Now, with this insightful and extremely helpful book, there is a resource for both managers and employees. Every business school should have MOBBING on the reading list, and every HR department should have it in the library.

—James A. Autry,
Author, *Love and Profit: the Art of Caring Leadership*

This ambitious, comprehensive volume defines the institutionalization of cruelty as "mobbing", comforts individuals with the reminder that they have options even when their work world and those in it feverishly attempt to destroy the kindest and brightest souls, and calls for all ancillary groups and institutions to stop the systematic destruction of the human spirit.

—Gary Namie, Ph.D,
Co-author of *The Bully at Work*

A strength of this work is that it drives home the point that being ganged up on has essentially the same effects, no matter what the nominal reasons.

While well-researched, comprehensive, and brilliant, this book is also engaging and easy to read, and enlivened on almost every page by first-person comments from people mobbed at work. Like my own students hearing this material in class, readers of this book will recognize, if not themselves, at least co-workers they have known.

With the publication of this book, once it is read, the worst should be over, and the rebuilding of a life can begin. For anybody mobbed at work, this book will be a healing gift.

—Kenneth Westhues, Ph.D.,
Author of *Eliminating Professors: A Guide to the Dismissal Process*

MOBBING should help to raise our consciousness about generic harassment and perhaps lead to worthwhile legislative and policy reforms. At the moment, the

continued...

U.S. public is focused on physical violence and tends to overlook workplace psychological abuse, so your book will be a much needed corrective.

—Richard V. Denenberg,
Author of *The Violence-Prone Workplace*

MOBBING is one of the most important books in understanding the dark side of life in organizations. What is alarming is that the incidents of mobbing behaviors appear to be on the increase, leading to greater despair in the work place and possible workplace violence.

—Edward S. Beck, Ed.D.,
Director Susquehanna Institute

I have already bought several copies of MOBBING for clients and have sent several copies to management in companies with whom I consult. I am considering providing a copy to every client I have who either is in, or is considering, employment litigation.

—C. Brady Wilson, Ph.D.,
Clinical Psychologist, Author of *Businesses Suffer from Workplace Trauma* (Article)

MOBBING -- A Must Read for Employment Lawyers.

—Scott H. Peters, Esq.,
The Peters Law Firm, P.C., Council Bluffs, Iowa

MOBBING is a valuable contribution to raising awareness of emotional abuse at work. Right now, people believe bullying and scapegoating and mobbing to be "the way the world works." With your help, it may eventually change.

—Chauncey Hare,
Therapist and Co-Author with Judith Wyatt of
Work Abuse: How to Recognize and Survive It

A life saver for workers unjustly kicked out! At first I balked at the term "mobbing." But as I read, I found the discussion of the mobbing phenomenon so accurately explaining what I had just experienced that I was able to pull out of the self-blame mode rather quickly. I see now that this book was a life-saver for me! Perhaps literally.

—Daniel G. Clark, Clark and Associates

MOBBING is excellent! I have seen numerous examples of "mobbing" in the workplace over the years and agree that it is devastating. Group craziness and lots of projections. What a mess. Great topic and great book! You are serving an important need.

—Tom Golden,
Author of *Swallowed by a Snake*

MOBBING brought Leymann's concepts to the New World.

—Newsweek, International Edition, August 14, 2000

MOBBING

Emotional Abuse in the American Workplace

Noa Davenport, Ph.D.
Ruth Distler Schwartz
Gail Pursell Elliott

Foreword by Dr. Heinz Leymann

Illustrations by Sabra Vidali

CIVIL SOCIETY PUBLISHING
AMES, IOWA

Published by
Civil Society Publishing
P.O. Box 1663
Ames, Iowa 50010-1663
www.mobbing-usa.com

Illustrations by Sabra Vidali
Book design by Laurel Albright and R.A. Schwartz & Associates
Cover design by R.A. Schwartz & Associates, Todd Emerson Hanson, Designer
Authors' photographs by Donna Andrews, Steven Alexander, James Jorn

Printed in the United States of America
First paperback edition 1999
Second printing 2002
ISBN 0-9671803-0-9

1. Mobbing in the workplace.   2. Bullying at work.   3. Employees, emotional
abuse of.   4. Work-stress.   5. Health.   6. Self-help.   7. Human resources
management.   8. Psychology, Industrial.   9. Labor law.   10. Business.
I. Title.

For book orders:
BookMasters, Inc.
P.O. Box 388
Ashland, OH 44805
(800) 247-6553
e-mail: order@bookmaster.com

This publication is designed to provide information in regard to the subject matter
covered. It is sold with the understanding that it is not a substitute for, or an alter-
native to, the services of any professional. The authors and the publisher have neither liability nor responsibility to any person or entity with respect to any alleged
or real loss or damage caused, directly or indirectly, by the information contained
in this book.

◆

We dedicate this book

To the memory of Heinz Leymann, Ph.D., M.D. sci.
who pioneered the research on workplace mobbing

and

To my husband, Aaron L. Davenport

To the memory of my mother, Eleanore Distler,
and to Clyde Schwartz and
my daughters Rebecca and Melissa

To my children, Derek and Blake Elliott

◆

PREFACE

This second printing differs from the first only in a few minor details: We changed some information no longer pertinent and added references to books and articles published since 1999.

Since the publication of MOBBING, we have received only positive feedback. We acknowledge the hundreds of persons who gratefully wrote to us. They confirmed that our initial intent to offer a self-help book was met.

Awareness is slowly growing in the U.S. and in Canada about the darker side of work and the devastating effects that mobbing and bullying can have on the self, health, organizations, and society. Our colleagues in North America, though still rather few, do their part to contribute to the growing interest.

Three conferences on the topic have been organized in the U.S. since 2000, in California, Massachusetts and Iowa; the Department of Environmental Quality for the State of Oregon has established the first anti-mobbing policy in the U.S.; efforts to add new anti-mobbing legislation are under way in California, other states and in Canada; and several new Internet self-help and advice groups and websites address specific professional groups or aspects of incivility at work. In the aftermath of the Columbine and other school shooting tragedies, the media have increasingly discussed bullying in the schools, thus raising awareness of adult bullying/mobbing in the workplace.

We continue to present about workplace mobbing to the media, corporations, and professional organizations; and act as expert witnesses in legal cases. And last but not least, our book has been used as required reading in several college courses.

Parallel to these developments in the U.S., pro-action keeps growing around the world. For example, a major international conference was held in early 2002 in Australia and a symposium on the topic is planned for 2004 in China. In January 2002, France enacted an anti-mobbing law; and most importantly, in Germany, workplace mobbing has been acknowledged in the medical establishment as an ill-making condition, and is recognized in the European Union as an occupational safety and health risk. Our book has raised interest in Japan and a Japanese edition is now available.

With these developments, we hope this second printing will help to keep the momentum going in North America and around the Globe.

◆ CONTENTS ◆

INTRODUCTION

Introduces the nature of the mobbing syndrome, informs about background of the research and the use of different terms.

PART I

CHAPTER 1: WHAT MOBBING IS AND HOW IT HAPPENS

Describes, analyzes and defines the syndrome. What mobbing entails. Mobbing behaviors. Degrees of mobbing and how it evolves over time. The role of management. Why mobbing is different from any other form of harassment or discrimination.

CHAPTER 2 — WHY MOBBING OCCURS AND PERSISTS

Presents reasons from different points of view and attempts to understand the phenomenon in the context of systems thinking. The personality of the instigators, group dynamics, links to workplace structures and the wider society. The role the victim may play in the mobbing. Why mobbing behaviors are allowed to persist.

PART II

CHAPTER 3 — HOW MOBBING AFFECTS YOU

Examines the devastating impact mobbing has on an individual's health and emotional well-being. Provides strategies to survive the experience without long term negative personal and professional repercussions.

CHAPTER 4 — HOW YOU CAN COPE

Advises victims of mobbing about helpful ways to overcome the experience.

CHAPTER 5 — FAMILY AND FRIENDS, HOW THEY ARE AFFECTED, HOW THEY CAN HELP

Describes the potential impact of mobbing on family, friends, and significant relationships. Explains the mobbed person's state of mind and how support can best be given.

PART III

CHAPTER 6 — How Mobbing Affects
the Organization —
Impact and Prevention, The Bottom Line

Discusses the impact on the organization. Offers suggestions for strategies to detect, halt and prevent mobbing from occurring. Recommends modifications to existing human resource policies and procedures.

PART IV

CHAPTER 7 — THE CHALLENGE OF CONFLICT RESOLUTION

Analyzes the triggering event—a conflict—of the mobbing syndrome. Discusses the apparent predicament of the attempt to resolve the conflict, why the attempt is often futile and what can be done about it.

CHAPTER 8 — MOBBING AND THE LAW

Addresses the legal framework as it currently can be used to address mobbing. Concludes with an appeal to lawmakers.

CHAPTER 9 — ACTING ON AWARENESS

Discusses implications and the cost of the mobbing syndrome to the American economy and society. Specifies the responsibility all sectors of the society have to deal with mobbing, and the role they play in helping to prevent mobbing.

AUTHORS' NOTE

This book came about because all three of us, in different organizations, experienced a workplace phenomenon that had profound effects on our well-being. Through humiliation, harassment, and unjustified accusations, we experienced emotional abuse that forced us out of the workplace.

As time went on, we discovered that this phenomenon not only had happened to us, and to some of our colleagues, but that it was a well-known occurrence in Europe. There it has been researched, documented and widely written about. Not until we discovered this literature did we understand that we had been victims of *workplace mobbing*. What we found described what had happened—in one form or another, to one degree or another—to each of us.

For the first time, a powerful image—*mobbing*—defined what we had experienced.

To our amazement, we found only limited information about this particular phenomenon in the United States. As we continued to discover other people who had experienced mobbing, we decided to collect their stories and present them in a book specifically addressed to the American audience.

We were most significantly inspired by Dr. Heinz Leymann, a German industrial psychologist and medical scientist who lived and worked in Sweden, where he first shed light on this phenomenon. He defined it, gave it a name, and since 1982, tirelessly researched and published about it in Sweden, Austria, Germany, France, United Kingdom, Japan and Australia. Our book builds on his work and expands upon his insights.

Our intent is to create more public awareness in the United States and to sound the alarm. We want to help detect mobbing in American workplaces, to warn those who intentionally perpetrate mobbing actions, and to encourage preventive, timely and appropriate action.

We believe that it is of the utmost urgency that America's workforce understands the nature, complexity and gravity of this syndrome. We want to say to the American worker: *There is a workplace syndrome called "mobbing." There are certain behaviors by your coworkers that can make you a victim of mobbing. You are not alone if this happens to you. There are ways to protect yourself.*

We want to tell responsible management, human resources personnel, unions, health care providers and insurance agencies: *There is a traumatic syndrome called "mobbing." The person who seems to be a "difficult" person, or has become mentally or physically ill, might very well be a victim of workplace mobbing.*

We offer suggestions to families and friends: *Your loved ones need your full support while they experience workplace mobbing. Understand that they are deeply injured. You can help.*

A massive public awareness campaign, stimulated by Dr. Leymann's research, particularly in Scandinavia and in German-speaking countries, has forced organizations to face the phenomenon of workplace mobbing. As a result, many people in Europe have found assistance and recourse.

This is what we hope this book will do in this country as well. We expect that it will stimulate new and more research. We expect new and appropriate legislation to protect people from being mobbed at the workplace and to increase their legal options. We expect new insights for appropriate medical treatment.

Above all, this is intended as a self-help book for victims of mobbing. We provide tools that will empower people to help themselves before it is too late, before their psychological and physical health is affected too gravely. And we hope that they will find the strength to move beyond their experience.

FOREWORD

This is the first book in the U.S. that presents the research of the last two decades on mobbing—also known as bullying—in a comprehensive way.

Though this phenomenon has been recognized among children, before 1982 it was totally unidentified as such in the work world of adults.

In order to identify the problem in the workplace, new research methodologies had to be developed. These did not focus on communication theories but looked at stress factors as used in occupational health. The research questions then became: If one can identify mobbing as an extreme form of psychological pressure, how much of this pressure can a normal human being withstand? At what point does mobbing result in illness? Where are the limits?

In the last two decades, much research has been done which has expanded our understanding of the causes and the effects of mobbing. This book presents this information in an excellent way. In particular, the sections that offer steps for action will be valuable help for the reader who is in pain.

Today, research is confronted with the challenge to produce more information about the after-effects of the victim's expulsion from the job. Following years of having been stigmatized, victims often do not see any possibilities to help themselves. They feel totally alone. Their social environment has been dissolved. They have no way to make a living. At this time, we do not yet know enough about these ramifications.

It is also important to engage in statistical studies to ascertain the extent of the working population affected by mobbing. Additionally important is research regarding these topics:

1. Which treatments are effective so that the person harmed through mobbing will not become chronically ill?

2. How can professional rehabilitation be achieved so that the victims can be reintegrated into the workforce?

3. How can legal protection for mobbing victims be strengthened?

4. How can people in a civil society be protected so that they do not become disaffected?

I wish this book much success because it is an important work. It sheds light on great suffering and proposes ideas to reduce this suffering.

Stockholm, December 1998
Dr. Heinz Leymann

INTRODUCTION
DRIVEN BEYOND ENDURANCE

Joan began having episodes of uncontrollable crying, and for the first time in her life, had anti-anxiety medication prescribed by her physician. A seasoned administrator, she had for months been forced to make decisions without complete information. Her decisions were then questioned or overturned. She was also forced to attend meetings where she was totally ignored. Unrealistic deadlines and a dramatically increased workload overwhelmed her. Furthermore, others in the organization undermined her authority. She resigned, with a negotiated settlement.

Sean, an experienced tradesman in a service organization, was excluded from meetings and cut off from information necessary to perform his job effectively. He was subjected to constant insults and his work was belittled. He was also forced to perform hazardous tasks without assistance, while supervisors or others watched. Consequently, he suffered a heart attack while on the job. Considered recovered, he returned to his job, but was fired soon after. He filed for unemployment compensation which was denied, appealed, and finally granted.

With more than 30 years of experience in management, Ron was a successful project leader in a high-tech company. A major project brought almost to fruition, he was suddenly relieved of his staff and responsibilities. His new supervisor began to assume full credit for his work. Isolated at a small desk, Ron no longer was included in any meetings or discussions. After a few months, he was found wandering the streets with blood streaming down his face. He had just walked into a wall. Later, following an emotional meeting with his superior, he suffered a heart attack, went on disability, and was unable ever to return to work.

Like Ron, Joan, and Sean, every year, millions of Americans become victims of emotional abuse inflicted at work. They are damaged to such an extent that they can no longer accomplish their tasks. Co-workers, colleagues, superiors, and subordinates attack their dignity, integrity and competence, repeatedly, over a number of weeks, months, or years. At the end, they resign, voluntarily or involuntarily, are terminated, or forced into early retirement. This is mobbing—workplace expulsion through emotional abuse.

Ironically, and sadly, the victims are portrayed as the ones at fault, as the ones who brought about their own downfalls. Mind you, Ron, Joan and Sean were not people who had a reputation of not performing well, not meeting organizational standards, or who could not get along with others. They were qualified. They had contributed their talents to the organization. They had been in the organization for a number of years.

How, you might ask, when there seem to be more structures and laws designed to protect workers than ever before, is this particular workplace behavior allowed to exist? There are three reasons.

One is that mobbing behaviors are ignored, tolerated, misinterpreted, or actually instigated by the company or the organization's management as a deliberate strategy.

The second reason is that this behavior has not yet been identified as a workplace behavior clearly different from sexual harassment or discrimination.

Thirdly, more often than not, the victims are worn down, feel destroyed and exhausted. They feel incapable of defending themselves, let alone initiating legal action.

MOBBING, BULLYING AND HARASSMENT
A BRIEF HISTORY OF THE RESEARCH

The word *mob* means a disorderly crowd engaged in lawless violence. It is derived from the Latin *mobile vulgus* meaning "vacillating crowd." The verb *to mob* means "to crowd about, attack or annoy."

In the sixties, the eminent Austrian ethologist Konrad Lorenz used the English term mobbing to describe the behavior that animals use to scare away a stronger, preying enemy. A number of weaker individuals crowd together and display attacking behavior, such as geese scaring away a fox.[1]

Later, Dr. Peter-Paul Heinemann, a Swedish physician, researched a behavior displayed by children and directed at other children, a behavior now generally called bullying. He used Lorenz's term "mobbing" to emphasize the seriousness of the behavior that could drive the victim to such isolation and despair that s/he committed suicide. The book was published in Sweden in 1972 with the title *Mobbing: Group Violence Among Children* (title translated).

In the eighties, Dr. Heinz Leymann used the term mobbing when he discovered similar group violence among adults at the workplace. He researched this behavior first in Sweden and then brought it to public awareness in Germany. He investigated what he was told were "difficult" people in the workplace and determined that many of these people were not "difficult" to begin with. He found that the root of their behavior was not a character flaw that made them inherently difficult. What he found was a work structure and culture that created the circumstances that marked these people as difficult. Once identified as difficult, the company created further reasons for terminating them. This, Leymann identified as mobbing.

In 1984, he published his first report regarding these findings. Since then, he published more than 60 research articles and books, such as *Mobbing: Psychoterror at the Workplace and How You Can Defend Yourself; The New Mobbing Report: Experiences and Initiatives, Ways Out and Helpful Advice.*[2]

Following Leymann's impetus, a great deal of research has been accomplished or is now in progress, particularly in Norway and Finland as well as in the UK, Ireland, Switzerland, Austria, Hungary, Italy, France, Australia, New Zealand, Japan, and South Africa.[3]

In the United States, as early as 1976, Dr. Carroll Brodsky, a psychiatrist and anthropologist, wrote *The Harassed Worker*. Brodsky wrote his book based on claims filed with the California Workers' Compensation Appeals Board and the Nevada Industrial Commission. These claims stated that the workers were "ill and unable to work because of ill-treatment by employers, co-workers, or consumers, or because of excessive demands for work output."[4]

He uses the term *harassment* as a behavior that "involves repeated and persistent attempts by one person to torment, wear down, frustrate, or get a reaction from another. It is behavior that persistently provokes, pressures, frightens, intimidates, or otherwise discomforts another person." Dr. Brodsky pointed out how crippling and pervasive the effects of harassment on mental health, physical health, and worker productivity were and expressed the belief that these claims were "only the tip of an iceberg in relation to the actual incidences."[5]

When Dr. Leymann first defined mobbing at the workplace in Sweden in 1984, he wrote that "mobbing was psychological terror" involving "hostile and unethical communication directed in a systematic way by one or a few individuals mainly towards one individual."

The person who is mobbed is pushed into a helpless and defenseless position. These actions occur on a very frequent basis and over a long period of time.[6]

Both Brodsky and Leymann stress the frequency and duration of what is done.

In 1988, Andrea Adams, a journalist, was the first person to draw attention to the bully phenomenon in the United Kingdom through a BBC series, and in 1992, her book *Bullying at Work: How to Confront and Overcome It* was published. Bullying in her use of the term is about "persistently finding fault" and "belittling individuals," often with a consenting management.

In 1997, a Trust named after Andrea Adams was created to assist victims of bullying. The trust commissioned research on the extent of bullying and abusive e-mails in the workplace. They found what they called an "explosion" of flame mail, or electronic bullying, sexist and racist abuse, including voice-mail.

Tim Field, another British author has written *Bully in Sight*. Published in 1996, it is a detailed handbook on how to identify and deal with bullies in the workplace. He defines *bullying* as a "continual and relentless attack on other people's self-confidence and self-esteem." The underlying reasons for this behavior is a desire to dominate, subjugate, and eliminate. Additionally, Field includes the perpetrator's denial of responsibility for any consequences of his or her actions.[7]

The term bullying is used in the United Kingdom and some English-speaking countries to identify many actions that Leymann terms as mobbing behaviors. It appears both terms are being used somewhat interchangeably. "What is meant by bullying and what is meant by mobbing is somewhat blurred at the moment," says Charlotte Rayner, a researcher on bullying behavior in the United Kingdom.[8]

In 1998, the International Labour Office (ILO) published the report, *Violence at Work,* written by Duncan Chappell and Vittorio Di Martino. In this report, mobbing and bullying behaviors are discussed alongside homicide and other more commonly known violent behaviors.[9]

THE U.S. AND CANADA

Although Dr. Carroll Brodsky's research on the harassed worker in 1976 recognized abusive workplace behavior, mobbing has not yet been widely identified as a workplace issue in the United States. However, it is now gradually being recognized.

Leymann's article *Mobbing and Psychological Terror* at Workplaces was published in the American journal *Violence and Victims in 1990.*[10]

In 1991 the *Personnel Journal* published an article by C. Brady Wilson, a clinical psychologist who specializes in workplace trauma, that pointed out the costs in billions of dollars that U.S. businesses are losing caused by real or perceived abuse of employees. "Workplace trauma, as psychologists refer to the condition caused by employee abuse, is emerging as a more crippling and devastating problem for employees and employers alike than all the other work-related stresses put together."[11]

Dr. Harvey A. Hornstein, professor of social-organizational psychology at Columbia University, wrote *Brutal Bosses and Their Prey: How to Identify and Overcome Abuse in the Workplace,* published in 1996. The brutal boss, in Hornstein's use of the term, is what Field and Adams call a bully. Both terms also imply physical assault.

A number of other North American academics have begun research in the last few years. In 1995, Lois Price Spratlen, University Ombudsman at the University of Washington, wrote an article on "Interpersonal Conflict Which Includes Mistreatment in a University Workplace" that was published in *Violence and Victims*. She defines *workplace mistreatment* "as a behavior or situations—without sexual or racial connotations—which the recipient perceives to be unwelcome, unwanted, unreasonable, inappropriate, excessive, or a violation of human rights."[12]

Dr. Loraleigh Keashly, Academic Director, graduate program in dispute resolution, College of Urban, Labor and Metropolitan Affairs at Wayne State University, uses the term *emotional abuse* in the workplace. She analyzes and summarizes North American research predominantly published in the eighties and nineties dealing with what she defines as "hostile verbal and nonverbal behaviors that are not explicitly tied to sexual or racial content yet are directed at gaining compliance from others."[13]

In 1998, Dr. Kenneth Westhues, professor of Sociology at the University of Waterloo, in Ontario, Canada, wrote a tongue-in-cheek book dealing with the horrors of academic mobbing entitled *Eliminating Professors: A Guide to the Dismissal Process*.[14]

Dr. Nicole Rafter, Northeastern University, Law, Policy and Society Program, began researching the mobbing phenomenon using the mobbing terminology in the early nineties.[15]

In the more popular literature too, an increasing number of publications identify the phenomenon. Examples are: Emily S. Bassmann's 1992 book, *Abuse in the Workplace*; and *Work Abuse: How to Recognize and Survive It*, by Judith Wyatt and Chauncey Hare (1997).

Also, there have been many stories reported in the media about bullying at the workplace that point to abusive work behaviors that we would now identify as mobbing. As an example, in November, 1998, Oprah Winfrey's show was dedicated to *Bully Bosses* and several persons told their stories in public.[16]

This growing awareness has led to the establishment of workplace help organizations, also on the Internet. One such organization, *The Campaign Against Workplace Bullying* (CAWB), led by Drs. Ruth and Gary Namie, is located in Bellingham, WA. Information on their organization and their 2000 book, *The Bully at Work!*, can be found on the web.[17] Also, Bob Rosner, author and syndicated columnist, gives advice to dissatisfied workers on the website *Working Wounded*.

Thousands more webpages can be found on the Internet under the word *bullying and mobbing* combined, although many deal with children's bullying behaviors. Dr. Leymann developed a webpage several years ago, and posted a great deal of important information on the identification, effect, and treatment of mobbing. This page continues to be updated by his colleagues.[18]

EXTENT OF MOBBING

Extensive research conducted in Sweden in 1990 extrapolated that 3.5 % of the labor force of 4.4 million persons, i.e. some 154,000, were mobbing victims at any given time.[19] Dr. Leymann also estimated that 15% of the suicides in Sweden are directly attributed to workplace mobbing.

If we transpose these figures to the U.S. workforce, comprising some 127 million people, well over 4 million people yearly are, or may become, victimized by mobbing. Hornstein, in his book *Brutal Bosses and Their Prey*, estimated that as many as 20 million Americans face workplace abuse on a daily basis—a near epidemic. [20] Dr. Carroll Brodsky told us, "It is not a near epidemic. It *is* an epidemic!"

Estimates of emotional assaults at work in other countries vary considerably. In the UK, for example, one researcher estimated that 50% of employees may be subjected to "bullying" at some time during their careers, whereas Leymann estimated that this figure is about 25% in Sweden.[21]

On the question of age, as an example, Leymann's research in Sweden suggests that mobbing happens slightly more to younger people in the age range of 21 to 40.[22] A study done in Norway found older workers had a higher risk of victimization than younger workers.[23] However, a study done in Switzerland in 1994 revealed that all age ranges were affected.[24]

The ability of older persons to find another job after a mobbing experience may be severely hampered, which means that he or she is, in effect, expelled from the labor market. This may be the key reason behind the finding in Sweden that those who developed post-traumatic stress disorder because of mobbing are rarely younger than 40 years of age.[25]

Other data from Germany indicate that mobbing affects professionals more frequently than workers.[26]

A great deal of research is needed to determine the extent of mobbing in the U.S., who the most likely targets may be, and which industries may be especially prone to mobbing.

WHAT IS BEING DONE ABOUT IT IN EUROPE

Because of the extensive literature and media coverage in Europe, the awareness of mobbing in the workplace is widespread. Mobbing has now become a household word in Scandinavia and in German-speaking countries.

Sweden, Norway, Finland and Germany have enacted new proactive and protective occupational safety laws, including emotional well-being, to legally address the mobbing behavior. For example, in 1993, the Swedish National Board of Occupational Safety and Health adopted an *Ordinance Concerning Victimization at Work*.

The ordinance contains provisions on measures against victimization at work and general recommendations on the implementation of the provisions. The ordinance defines victimization as "recurrent and reprehensible or distinctly negative actions which are directed against individual employees in an offensive manner and can result in those employees being placed outside the workplace community."[27]

Furthermore, the Ordinance states that "employees who are subjected to victimization shall quickly be given help or support. The employer shall have special procedures for this."[28]

Another example of a proactive approach comes from Germany. It is an agreement that the Board of the Hamburg University Hospital made with the hospital personnel board in July of 1997. The agreement refers to the establishment of an internal and confidential center *to inform, consult, educate, assist, and mediate in mobbing cases.*[29]

New legislation is being proposed in the United Kingdom and Australia as well.

In addition, new organizations have been created to help victims of mobbing. Measures have been initiated in a relatively brief time period to deal with mobbing behaviors, help mobbing victims, and help prevent further mobbing from occurring. For example, telephone hotlines have been installed in Switzerland, Austria, Germany, and in the UK. Contact addresses for receiving counseling or advice have been published in the daily press.

The need for rehabilitation of mobbing victims has been so widespread that Dr. Leymann established a special clinic in Sweden. However, it ceased to operate due to lack of support by the National Health Insurance Agency. Dr. Leymann had treated some 1700 mobbing patients, mainly in Germany, Sweden, and Norway. Together with Dr. Michael Becker, a German psychiatrist and neurologist, he also developed a special treatment protocol.

These examples of proaction are what we envision for this country.

◆

This book raises awareness of the mobbing syndrome as a serious workplace issue dealing with emotional mistreatment of employees, most often leading to voluntary or involuntary resignation or dismissal. People who have been affected by mobbing are suffering immensely.

We chose to talk about *mobbing* and the *mobbing syndrome* rather than bullying, a term that invokes individual acts of aggression. Mobbing, on the other hand, entails emotional abuse committed directly or indirectly by a group. Furthermore, bullying is often used when referring to children who bully other children in the school environment. We want to clearly identify mobbing as an abusive group behavior committed in the workplace.

We trust that employees will not use this information as an excuse when they face dismissal or reprimand because of other, well grounded reasons, and falsely name it mobbing. And, although this book focuses on the prevalence of the mobbing syndrome, there are many organizations in this country that are run by outstanding leaders who would never tolerate mobbing behaviors in their organizations.

OUR INTERVIEW PARTNERS

Our interview partners have all been individuals with a great deal of experience. Our sample consists predominantly of professionals in their forties and fifties, although some individuals were in their thirties when mobbing began. Some had more than one graduate degree. We interviewed women and men who had worked in nonprofit organizations, in major companies, in universities, in the healthcare industry. They came from different parts of the country and were of different ethnic origins.

With some we talked for hours, with others less. Some are still enduring the trauma; others related their insights as a result of introspection. Throughout the book, real incidents of mobbing are described in their words.

We identify our interview partners with fictitious names and we altered the description of their workplaces. We do not identify our interview partners' age, gender, race, religion, or ethnicity, etc., when we quote them throughout the text. By choosing to do this, we want to emphasize that these classifications really do not matter in a mobbing, as mobbing is not an aggressive act against someone belonging to a protected class but emotional assaults directed at *anybody*.

Introduction Endnotes

1. Lorenz, Konrad, 1963. Das sogenannte Boese. Zur Naturgeschichte der Aggression. Wien. Page 41. Lorenz, Konrad, 1991. Here Am I Where Are You? The Behavior of the Greylag Goose. New York.

2. Both books are published in German, see bibliography.

3. For comprehensive research overviews see: Zapf, Dieter and Leymann, Heinz: "Foreword" in: Mobbing and Victimization at Work. European Journal of Work and Organizational Psychology. 1966, 5 (2), p.181. A first empirical analysis by Klaus Niedl of mobbing in Austria was published in German in 1995. It also contains a good summary, primarily of the Scandinavian research. Another research review, in English, is an introduction to Stale Einarsen's and Anders Skogstad's study "Bullying at Work: Epidemiological Findings in Public and Private Organizations." In: European Journal of Work and Organizational Psychology, 1996, 5 (2), 185-201. Loraleigh Keashly summarized studies on workplace emotional abuse in her article "Emotional Abuse in the Workplace: Conceptual and Empirical Issues," published in the Journal of Emotional Abuse, Vol.1 (1) in 1998. In 1999 Helge Hoel, Charlotte Rayner and Cary L. Cooper offered a comprehensive review and analysis of the literature in their article "Workplace Bullying" in the International Review of Industrial and Organizational Psychology, Vol. 14, 195-230. Furthermore, a German researcher, Harald Ege, has done extensive research in Italy and published his work in Italian. See website: www.mobbing-prima.it.

4. Brodsky, 1976:xi.

5. Brodsky, 1976:2.

6. Leymann, 1996:168.

7. Field, 1996:33.

8. Personal communication.

9. Duncan Chappell and Vittorio Di Martino, Violence at Work, International Labour Office, 1998.

10. Violence and Victims, Vol. 5.2., pp. 119-125.

11. Wilson, Brady C. 1991: p. 47.

12. Price Spratlen, 1995:287.

13. Loraleigh Keashly, Emotional Abuse in the Workplace: Conceptual and Empirical Issues. In: Journal of Emotional Abuse, Vol. 1 (1) 1998, p. 85-117.

14. Westhues, 1998. Dr. Kenneth Westhues has also written a thorough case analysis about an academic mobbing: Human Sacrifice in Universities: Toronto versus Richardson (proposed title, forthcoming 2002).

15. Dr. Nicole Rafter has done numerous in-depth interviews with targets of mobbing.

16. November 24, 1998, The Oprah Winfrey Show, Bully Bosses.

17. The Campaign Against Workplace Bullying <www.bullybusters.org>.

18. The Mobbing Encyclopedia, <www.leymann.se>.

19. Leymann 1995:19.

20. Hornstein, 1996.

21. Hoel et. al. state in their 1999 article: "International comparisons are difficult to establish as there are subtle but important differences in operational definition used in these countries." 1999:198.

22. Leymann, 1996:175.

23. Stale Einarsen and Anders Skogstad: Bullying at Work: Epidemiological Findings in Public and Private Organizations. In: *European Journal of Work and Organizational Psychology*, 1996, 5 (2), 185-201.

24. Schuepbach, Torre, 1996:152.

25. Leymann & Gustafsson, 1996.

26. Grund, 1995:96.

27. Statute Book of the Swedish National Board of Occupational Safety and Health. Ordinance (AFS 1993:17). *Victimization at Work*, Section 1.

28. Statute Book of the Swedish National Board of Occupational Safety and Health. Ordinance (AFS 1993:17). *Victimization at Work*, Section 6. Swedish National Board of Occupational Safety and Health, S-171 84 Solna, Sweden. Tel. + 46 8 730 9000; Fax + 46 8 730 1967.

29. Dienstvereinbarung: Anlaufstelle zur Loesung von Konflikten am Arbeitsplatz. Universitaets-Krankenhaus Eppendorf, Martinistrasse 52, D-20246 Hamburg.

ONE

What Mobbing Is and How It Happens

When I say that evil has to do with killing, I do not mean to restrict myself to corporal murder. Evil is also that which kills spirit.

—M. Scott Peck
People of the Lie: The Hope for Healing Human Evil

♦

Mobbing is an emotional assault. It begins when an individual becomes the target of disrespectful and harmful behavior. Through innuendo, rumors, and public discrediting, a hostile environment is created in which one individual gathers others to willingly, or unwillingly, participate in continuous malevolent actions to force a person out of the workplace.

These actions escalate into abusive and terrorizing behavior. The victim feels increasingly helpless when the organization does not put a stop to the behavior or may even plan or condone it.

As a result, the individual experiences increasing distress, illness, and social misery. Frequently, productivity is affected and victims begin to use sick leave to try to recover from the daily pressures and torment. Depression or accidents may occur. Resignation, termination, or early retirement, the negotiated voluntary or involuntary expulsion from the workplace, follows.

For the victim, death—through illness or suicide—may be the final chapter in the mobbing story.

For the organization, mobbing is like a cancer. Beginning with one malignant cell, it can spread quickly, destroying vital elements of the organization. Remedial action must be taken at an early stage.

AGGRESSION AGAINST "ANYONE": WORKPLACE EXPULSION

Mobbing is aggression against "anyone"—rather than specific discrimination against someone based on age, gender, race, creed, nationality, disability or pregnancy—using harassing, abusive and often terrorizing behaviors. Mobbing is done intentionally to force the person out of the workplace.

Two different types of such malevolent conduct can be identified: active aggression and passive aggression. These tactics vary according to the subtlety of the aggressor. Passive aggressives are a special problem, since they can wrap their malevolence in acts of occasional kindness and politeness.

INJURY NOT ILLNESS

The psychological consequences of mobbing should be termed an injury not an illness, thus attributing the cause of the suffering to the persons who intentionally inflicted the harm.[1]

MOBBING TYPOLOGY

Dr. Heinz Leymann identified 45 mobbing behaviors and grouped them in five different categories, depending on the nature of the behavior. See boxes on the following pages. Not all of these will happen in every case.[2]

Any one of these behaviors, taken alone, may be despicable, uncivilized, and generally not acceptable. Any one, by itself, could possibly be tolerated as a sometime occurrence, or brushed off by assuming that a person doing such a thing might be having a bad day. And who has not? However, when these behaviors are displayed continuously and in many different variations, they become intentional abuse and create terror.

In the U.S., some of the discriminatory behaviors mentioned in category three, and any of the outright physical assault behaviors mentioned in category five, are illegal and are covered by laws in all 50 states. They would be, taken by themselves, ample grounds if the affected persons wanted to file a law suit. The majority of behaviors in categories one, two and four fall into behaviors that are considered within any employer's prerogative. Although considered management of the worst kind, there is no basis, as yet, that would allow one to build a legal case. Exceptions are: oral or written threats, and management that orders colleagues not to speak with you. Should you be given meaningless tasks to do or ones that are below your qualifications, this could be construed as another prerogative of the employer.

LEYMANN'S TYPOLOGY

First Category
Impact On Self-Expression and the Way Communication Happens

1. Your superior restricts the opportunity for you to express yourself.
2. You are interrupted constantly.
3. Colleagues/co-workers restrict your opportunity to express yourself.
4. You are yelled at and loudly scolded.
5. Your work is constantly criticized.
6. There is constant criticism about your private life.
7. You are terrorized on the telephone.
8. Oral threats are made.
9. Written threats are sent.
10. Contact is denied through looks or gestures.
11. Contact is denied through innuendoes.

Second Category
Attacks On One's Social Relations

1. People do not speak with you any more.
2. You cannot talk to anyone, i.e., access to others is denied.
3. You are put into a workspace that is isolated from others.
4. Colleagues are forbidden to talk with you.
5. You are treated as if you are invisible.

Third Category
Attacks On Your Reputation

1. People talk badly behind your back.
2. Unfounded rumors are circulated.
3. You are ridiculed.
4. You are treated as if you are mentally ill.

5. You are forced to undergo a psychiatric evaluation/examination.
6. A handicap is ridiculed.
7. People imitate your gestures, walk, voice to ridicule you.
8. Your political or religious beliefs are ridiculed.
9. Your private life is ridiculed.
10. Your nationality is ridiculed.
11. You are forced to do a job that affects your self-esteem.
12. Your efforts are judged in a wrong and demeaning way.
13. Your decisions are always questioned.
14. You are called demeaning names.
15. Sexual innuendoes.

Fourth Category
Attacks On the Quality of One's Professional and Life Situation

1. There are no special tasks for you.
2. Supervisors take away assignments, so you cannot even invent new tasks to do.
3. You are given meaningless jobs to carry out.
4. You are given tasks that are below your qualifications.
5. You are continuously given new tasks.
6. You are given tasks that affect your self-esteem.
7. You are given tasks that are way beyond your qualifications, in order to discredit you.
8. Causing general damages that create financial costs to you.
9. Damaging your home or workplace.

Fifth Category
Direct Attacks On a Person's Health

1. You are forced to do a physically strenuous job.
2. Threats of physical violence are made.
3. Light violence is used to threaten you.
4. Physical abuse.
5. Outright sexual harassment.

MOBBING AS A PROCESS

It is important to stress that mobbing happens as a process of abusive behaviors inflicted over time. It begins insidiously, and soon gains such momentum that a point of no return is reached. Like a tornado, the events escalate into a spiral. So what exactly does happen when mobbing occurs?

Leymann distinguishes five phases in the mobbing process.

Phase 1 is characterized by a critical incident, a *conflict*. In itself, this is not yet mobbing. It can, however develop into mobbing behaviors.

Phase 2 is characterized by *aggressive acts* and psychological assaults that set the mobbing dynamics into motion.

Phase 3 then *involves management* that plays a part in the negative cycle by misjudging the situation if they have not already been participating in phase 2. Instead of extending support, they begin the isolation and expulsion process.

Phase 4 is critical, as victims are now *branded as difficult or mentally ill*. This misjudgment by management and health professionals reinforces the negative cycle. It almost always will lead to expulsion or forced resignation.

Phase 5 is the *expulsion*. The trauma of this event can, additionally, trigger post-traumatic stress disorder (PTSD). After the expulsion, the emotional distress and the ensuing psychosomatic illnesses continue and often intensify.[3] (See Chapter 3.)

THE FIVE PHASES IN THE MOBBING PROCESS

1. Conflict
2. Aggressive Acts
3. Management Involvement
4. Branding as Difficult or Mentally Ill
5. Expulsion

DEGREES OF MOBBING

We have found it helpful to distinguish three major degrees of mobbing—first, second, and third—according to the different effects mobbing has on an individual. In analogy to the different degrees of injuries suffered from burning, the distinction indicates how deeply a person has been "burned" or "scarred" by the experience.

We do not use a scientific scale to assess these degrees but rather the different effects this experience had on us and our interview partners. The degrees are determined by a number of factors. In addition to the intensity, duration, and frequency of the mobbing, the psychology of the mobbed individuals, their upbringing, past experiences, and general circumstances are also considered. The scale only indicates how people can be affected differently by similar experiences.

Mobbing of the first degree: The individual manages to resist, escapes at an early stage, or is fully rehabilitated in the same workplace or somewhere else.

Mobbing of the second degree: The individual cannot resist, nor escape immediately, and suffers temporary or prolonged mental and/or physical disability, and has difficulty re-entering the workforce.

Mobbing of the third degree: The affected person is unable to re-enter the workforce. The physical and mental injuries are such that rehabilitation seems unlikely, unless a very specialized treatment protocol is being applied.[4]

It goes without saying that concepts such as prolonged, temporary, or frequent cannot usefully be quantified. The only measure of the intensity is the subjective assessment by the targeted individual. What clearly feels like mobbing to one person may not yet be considered as such by someone else. This will be discussed in more detail in Chapter 3.

THE MOBBING SYNDROME

In the following paragraphs, we describe the elements of the mobbing process and how it manifests itself in more detail. As mobbing comprises numerous factors that occur in combination and severely affect an individual's health, we chose to call it the mobbing syndrome. We define it as follows.

> The mobbing syndrome is a malicious attempt to force a person out of the workplace through unjustified accusations, humiliation, general harassment, emotional abuse, and/or terror.
>
> It is a "ganging up" by the leader(s)—organization, superior, co-worker, or subordinate—who rallies others into systematic and frequent "mob-like" behavior.
>
> Because the organization ignores, condones or even instigates the behavior, it can be said that the victim, seemingly helpless against the powerful and many, is indeed "mobbed." The result is always injury—physical or mental distress or illness and social misery and, most often, expulsion from the workplace.

TEN KEY FACTORS
OF THE MOBBING SYNDROME

The mobbing syndrome contains ten distinctive factors that occur in various combinations, systematically, and frequently. The impact of these factors on the targeted person then becomes the major element of the mobbing syndrome.

1. Assaults on the dignity, integrity, credibility, and professional competence of employees.

2. Negative, humiliating, intimidating, abusive, malevolent, and controlling communication.

3. Committed directly, or indirectly, in subtle or obvious ways.

4. Perpetrated by one or more staff members—"vulturing."

5. Occurring in a continual, multiple, and systematic fashion, over some time.

6. Portraying the victimized person as being at fault.

7. Engineered to discredit, confuse, intimidate, isolate, and force the person into submission.

8. Committed with the intent to force the person out.

9. Representing the removal from the workplace as the victim's choice.

10. Not recognized, misinterpreted, ignored, tolerated, encouraged, or even instigated by the management of the organization.

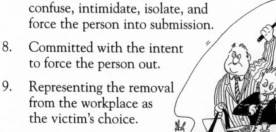

The combination of these ten major factors impacts gravely the emotional and physical well-being of the targeted individual and can result in death by illness, accident, or suicide.

The only remedy for this course of events is prevention, detection, early warning, and timely action.

In the following we discuss the ten factors further. Each is illustrated with quotes from different stories, and the behaviors are analyzed in more detail.

1. Assaults on the dignity, integrity, credibility, and professional competence

Joan: *I've been in business for twenty-seven years. I had never been anywhere where my ability, my credentials, my integrity were questioned.*

Catherine: *For the first time in my professional career, some-one was doubting my competence and curtailing my initiative. It was beyond my understanding.*

Carol described one of her co-workers that set the mob-bing process into motion: *He was also trying to ruin my reputation. He was always badmouthing me behind my back. Not knowing what he was doing and saying about me was one of the scariest things.*

Luis was the CEO of a nonprofit organization when he was mobbed by his vice president: *The rumor had been spread that I had had several small strokes and was in the beginnings of Alzheimer's disease and was no longer competent and able to lead the organization.*

As illustrated, mobbing comprises behaviors that rob individuals of their reputation, professional integrity, and competence. When professional competence is questioned, it also means that the individuals cannot be trusted. If they cannot be trusted, then in their perception, their work becomes worthless and they become worthless. **The effect is a loss of sense of self. This element, above all else, begins the mobbing cycle.**

2. Negative, humiliating, intimidating, abusive, malevolent, and controlling communication

Diana: *The perpetrator's aim is to scare everyone else into submission by attacking the victim, subtly or openly. Control reached in this way then allows the attacker to change his or her approach to one of benevolence, giving raises to the chosen few who participated in the mobbing.*

All others, including the chosen, believe the bloodletting is over and they are safe. This works for a while until the perpetrator needs to once again exert public control.

Judy: *I had worked with these vendors for fifteen years and considered them friends. When my new boss came, he brought these people into his office individually and told them that they were not to have contact with me. They were only to deal with him, even though he never would meet with them. And then he would denigrate me to them. When John, one of these vendors, came out of that office, his face was just pale. He couldn't believe it. And he told me, "You won't believe what he just said."*

Negative communication is aggressive communication intended to humiliate and degrade the person, often for one's own aggrandizement. Typical behaviors that can be called negative communication, as our interview partners experienced them, are:

- Laughing in your face.
- Making inappropriate jokes about you.
- Creating rumors or prejudice.
- Developing a fabricated case against your character.
- Denigrating your professional abilities.
- Withholding information necessary to do the job.
- Isolating you physically or socially.
- Holding meetings about your work, without your presence.
- Changing rules and regulations frequently.
- Controlling all in and outgoing correspondence.
- Requesting tasks that are difficult to accomplish in the given time frame.
- Taking away responsibility and giving the task to a less qualified person.
- Intense aggressive behavior, like yelling, slamming of doors and fists pounded on a table.
- Repeated calls at night requesting irrelevant information.

Joan: *I said to the director of Human Resources at one point, "I am totally isolated." And he said, malevolently, "That's the idea... isn't it?" He said to me on another occasion, "You know, a lot of people in your position might consider suicide." My response was, "That is a permanent solution to a temporary problem. But I can understand how someone might consider it."*

Clearly, the quoted director of Human Resources is insensitive, inexperienced, unethical, and malicious. He is displaying abusive, humiliating behavior.

Judy: *One day when I came into my office, he was in there whispering to my secretary. I knew they were talking*

about me. He said: "Is she too stupid to use a phone
book?" I was calling directory assistance because that
particular number was not in the phone book. I said: "I
cannot believe you are saying this. What kind of a mes-
sage does that send?" Then he started screaming at me.

It is not unusual that occasionally, even at the workplace, we
might laugh at someone or make fun of a person. Among friends, this
may be harmless. Many TV sitcoms feature this behavior over and
over again, actually demonstrating how well people get along. In a
different context, depending on the effect and the intent, jokes
can be demeaning, unwelcome, and can contribute to emotional
distress. An example of a malevolent and abusive behavior is what
Sean described.

Sean: *I had taken three days off for surgery and recuperation.*
I continually received pages and phone calls at my
home by both staff and managers asking me to come in
to plunge toilets and fix things.

Robert: *She tried to tarnish my name. She opened my mail,*
all correspondence. She would go behind my back and
talk to different representatives of the agencies that I
would normally deal with one-on-one, telling them
what a bad job I was doing and that I was not
supposed to be in that position. She gave me a bad
performance evaluation.

What else would she do? She would go into my office
and go through my desk, to check what I was doing. She
was trying to get into my computer, too, but she didn't
succeed. I would put some things on a disk and bring it
home. She tried to sabotage one major project that I
organized. It turned out very well anyway. But she
tried to sabotage it. And she wouldn't put through my
paperwork on some projects, so I didn't get paid in time.

45

3. **Committed directly, or indirectly, in subtle or obvious ways**

Jack: *The first thing he did was terminate the store manager. I was the assistant at this point. There was another assistant that he took into his confidence. They met daily and excluded me from everything that was going on.*

Neil: *There were weeks where I would not see my new boss. Previously I attended all the directors meetings, but I was not invited to them anymore. It was very weird. It bothered me at first, and then I rationalized to myself that there were other things that I could do. I just sat down and thought about it. What did it mean? How long could it last? And what could I do?*

Catherine: *I thought, "Why all these closed door meetings all of a sudden?" Before the new CEO came, rarely had I seen a closed door meeting in our organization.*

Our interview partners mentioned the following behaviors:

- No help is extended.
- Promises are made and not kept.
- No eye contact is made with you.
- Contact is minimized or avoided all together.
- You are ignored.
- Gestures that signal humiliation.
- Talking behind your back.
- Putting you in a room without a telephone.
- Communication via memos or e-mail about issues formerly discussed face-to-face.
- Denying contact with the public/media, when previously that was a part of the job.

- Having your work checked by someone unqualified to do so.

- Job descriptions changed without your knowledge.

- Policies changed or not followed.

- Mixed messages.

- You are made to look inconsistent.

- You are set up.

- Those supportive of you are discredited.

- An environment of paranoia is created.

- Removal or reduction of responsibility and authority.

- Replacing meaningful work with work that is humiliating or demeaning.

- Giving tasks you have not been adequately prepared to assume.

- Attacks on your private life.

4. Perpetrated by one or more staff members— "vulturing"

The perpetrator creates his or her circle of allies—the "mob." One person can begin the process and others join in.

> Diana: *When someone creates this environment, a strange thing comes over people. Because the victim is now seen as vulnerable, others join in, like vultures circling a carcass, and "pick" at the person. I call this "vulturing."*
>
> *Sometimes people participate out of fear of losing their position if they don't go along with the leader. But often there is an element of glee. They seem to be enjoying the vulnerability of the victim.*
>
> *In my company, everyone was worried about their own job since the arrival of the new CEO. I accepted their lack of support—and even some of their vulturing activities towards me—because of this.*
>
> *But I still find it incomprehensible that they, basically good people, participated as much as they did. Why weren't they outraged by the CEO's treatment of staff? Why weren't they repulsed and sickened? My body language could not hide my outrage at his abusive behavior toward others. I believe that's why his focus turned to me.*

The principal mobber can be the CEO, supervisor, or an equal in the workplace hierarchy, as well as a subordinate. Mobbing, therefore, as seen from an organizational chart, can be *vertical*, directed up as well as down, or it can be *horizontal*.

Mobbing behavior is quite often assumed by a new CEO to "whip the troops into line" or by a supervisor towards a new employee to "destroy any potential overthrow." When co-workers are attacking colleagues of the same hierarchical level, they may be jealous or fearful. In a competitive environment, they proceed to mob in the hope that their job will be maintained. When subordinates mob a superior, they may resent not having been included in decision-making about impending changes, or they may covet that person's job.

Jackie, an outside consultant in Luis' organization in which he was the president, observed what was going on within the organization.

> Jackie: *My office was next to the Senior Vice President's. It soon became clear to me that he was putting together a power base of employees, and I tried to tell the president that...I told him I felt he should be very careful, but he wasn't concerned. The Senior VP began to cultivate the most powerful board members and the most vocal. Since the president liked to keep a low profile, and trusted the Senior VP, he allowed him to do that.*

It would appear that the prevalence of a mobbing direction—vertically or horizontally—is correlated with the nature of a company culture and its preference of hierarchical structures. The more hierarchical, the more mobbing occurs vertically; the flatter the organization, the more mobbing happens horizontally.

Following is a very poignant example of vertically mobbing down. The image brings to mind total humiliation.

> Sean: *The Vice President told me to start ripping up the existing carpet. Disabled people were in the home, and one of them was walking around us at the time. Please understand that the staff at this home had not cleaned the carpet in weeks, although I had pointed out its condition to them as well as management staff, and brought them the carpet cleaner to use.*
>
> *The carpet was filthy and soaked in spots from urine. I pointed this out to him, saying that it would be hazardous to start ripping it up while the people were in the home and suggested that we wait until they were removed, arrangements the staff were hurriedly trying to make.*

He told me again to just start ripping it up, which I did.
Another supervisor was with him and said nothing. They
then both stood there and watched me while I started the
work. It required tearing up carpet that had been glued to
the floor, which is a tough job. As I said, it was filthy,
soaked with urine all the way through, which had left the
glue a gooey mess in places, and created dust and debris.
They stood there and watched me in silence for some
time. They did not offer to help move furniture or people
out of the way. This was not the first time this type of
thing had happened.

What Diana calls "vulturing" is often involved in the creation of the "mob." It gives people the justification to act out, or do what they otherwise would not.

5. Occurring in a continual, multiple, and systematic fashion over some time

Jeff: *I started getting district manager visits. I mean very*
frequently. Before that time, it was probably every six
or eight weeks. Then it started to be as frequent as
once a week.

Diana: *Every day was like going into battle. I never knew*
when the next bomb would be dropped. I was afraid to
trust anyone for fear they were the enemy. I tried to be
prepared at all times, but it was hopeless. My physical
and mental reserves were depleted. I knew I had to have
relief soon—but there was no letup.

It is the frequency, the repetitiveness, and duration that affects the victims most of all. The more intense the mobbing gets and the longer it lasts, the deeper the victim is affected. However, as described earlier, each person has a different tolerance level. What is still bearable for one person has already contributed to major injury in another.

6. Portraying the victimized person as being at fault

Although individuals had been performing at a high level, all of a sudden they are portrayed as incompetent, or faults are found that have not been a cause for complaints previously.

> Joan: *They were keeping a file, and they were not allowing me to address issues within my own area. When I said, "Why wasn't this brought to my attention?" They would say, "Well, the person was afraid to bring it to you." Or, "The person was afraid of retaliation." Or, "The person said they had already approached you with this and you did nothing."*
>
> *And I knew nothing about any of these concerns, or if I did, I was told by my direct subordinates that the situation had been handled satisfactorily. I believed them. But my department was beginning to fall apart because no one was addressing these issues. It snowballed.*
>
> *After I was gone, someone from another area was brought in and shredded most of the files in my office. They dissolved all of my systems and all of my procedures and tried to make it look like my area was a disaster and that it was my fault.*

Mobbing affects the victim's health. The mobbees begin to display a number of symptoms: loss of concentration, which impacts their performance; frequent absence due to illness, which impacts the organization. The mobbee is now at fault. And so the organization has grounds to terminate employment, engage in constructive discharge procedures, or force a resignation.

7. Engineered to discredit, confuse, intimidate, isolate, and force the person into submission

> Joan: *I did not know what was happening, or the seriousness of what was happening. It was confusing. You suddenly seem to be getting it from every direction possible.*

51

Jack: *I was taken off special projects that I had always done. Because I had been there so long and had so much experience, I had always been used as a resource. Now people were told not to do that any longer. Other stores who used to call were directed to call other people, forcing me into being an outsider. Isolating me.*

Initially, I really started to question whether I was doing my job right, whether I was still able to perform the right way. Before that point I had received a lot of praise, a lot of compliments on things, and I really had to adjust and find different ways to find out whether I was doing my job or not.

Co-workers and management publicly engage in acts of humiliation. This clearly leads to the expulsion phase.

8.   Committed with the intent to force the person out

Jack: *In this organization, managers rarely are terminated because policy provides a severance package when that occurs. The ones that leave on their own don't receive anything. So there is this unwritten way of getting rid of people. That was the reason I left Human Resources ten years ago. There were way too many times I was directed to do this to others. It was just too hard to do it anymore.*

Luis' wife: *What confounds me most of all is that this happened when Luis had such an outstanding record as the company president.*

While we were out of town, Luis was sent a retroactive termination. When we returned, we found his entire office cleared out. Someone had gone through every-thing—drawers, closets, took everything off the walls, loaded it into boxes, and left it outside the garage door at our home, without a note, telephone call, nothing. We came back from being out of town and found it.

Nothing illustrates the evil of this behavior so obviously—your office belongings, packed in boxes, at your doorsteps.

9. Representing the removal from the workplace as the victim's choice to leave

Joan: *I was going to file a lawsuit. But I signed an agreement not to sue in exchange for my resignation and a severance package.*

Ron: *I was 55 at the time and eligible for early retirement, but I didn't want to leave. I could have taken it to court and fought it, with 15 years of superior evaluations on my record.*

But, when you lay down the chips, you are better off taking retirement. A company this size hires its lawyers by the year, and they are tickled to death to go to court. And they will string it out for 50 years, if you are still around that long. This company doesn't lose very many cases. In fact, I know of several cases, but the company never lost any of them. The employee doesn't have the finances to fight it on and on and on. And the lawyers are just looking for a place to light.

As mentioned earlier, with his project taken away and now isolated and ignored, Ron suffered a massive heart attack following a disagreement with his new superior. He left his employer on total disability, never to return. (When we interviewed Ron, it had been more than 14 years since his encounter with mobbing. Yet, as he quietly recounted his experience, tears flowed freely down his face.)

10. Mobbing is not recognized, or is misinterpreted, ignored, tolerated, encouraged or even instigated by the top management of the organization

Jack: *He wasn't telling me this as a supervisor but as a friend. He was taking a risk telling me what really was going on. He said, "This pressure is going to come down on you. I have no choice in the matter. I have to do it, and I just want you to know that."*

The bottom line was—I was getting too old, 44 years, and making too much money. They could bring in two or three younger people for the same money.

A supervisor who first warned me about this four years before had been directed to lower my performance appraisals, and to implement disciplinary action. But he refused. And it's really unfortunate. He was then the one they went after and put on disciplinary action. Totally unfounded.

When we asked Robert about how he tried to get help in his situation, and what he did with the bad performance evaluations that he had received from his mobbing boss, he said:

I did not sign them, I did not agree with them. I questioned them at a higher level, but nothing was done. I went to her boss, and I went to the boss above that one, to the assistant director. And then to his boss, to the director. He just said, "I cannot believe this is happening." And nothing was ever done. This went on for five years.

This last factor, i.e., management ignores or even instigates the mobbing, promotes the syndrome most of all. The cycle of mobbing has begun. A conflict has escalated to a seemingly intractable situation and there are no avenues available for the person to find recourse: to explain, to be heard, to receive an apology or constructive suggestions as to how the problem could be resolved in a mutual agreement.

CONCLUSION

Morally, even if the victim has demonstrated some type of behavior which might have played a part in triggering the mobbing, there should be, in every organization or company, regulations, policies, and procedures in place that provide for hearing concerns, and for taking appropriate and helpful action, as we show in Chapter 6.

In sexual or racial discrimination or harassment, the affected person has legal recourse. U.S. laws protect citizens against these behaviors. But mobbing is a more generic form of abuse and does not readily fall under the protection of Civil Rights laws. The employer, or staff, can operate in a gray area. Some states, however, have a provision under the Workers' Compensation Law that provides for compensation for psychological trauma suffered on the job, legally referred to as *mental-mental* injury. This is presented in Chapter 8, *Mobbing and the Law*.

◆

Chapter 1 Endnotes

1. Tim Field in his book *Bully in Sight*, also insists on the term injury.

2. Leymann 1993:33,34, translated/adapted from German by N.D.

3. Leymann, 1996:171.

4. We refer to Dr. Leymann's treatment protocol published on the Internet as well as Wyatt and Hare's advice in *Work Abuse, How to Recognize and Survive It*.

5. In the Swedish research, Leymann found that horizontal mobbing, among peers, occurred in 44% of the cases. Mobbing vertically down, from supervisors directed at subordinates, occurred in 37% of the cases. And mobbing vertically up, attacking supervisors, occurred in 9% of cases. In 10% of cases, a combination of vertically down and horizontally occurred (Leymann, 1993:47). In a Swiss study, it was found that vertically mobbing down was more prevalent (Schuepbach, Torre, 1996:152).

◆ TWO ◆

Why Mobbing Occurs and Persists

This is a turbulent time for organizations. The changing characters of competition, downsizing, workforce demographics, customer demands, and popular images of leadership serve to either ignite abuse in otherwise reasonable bosses or unleash it from predisposed organizational bullies.

—Harvey Hornstein
Brutal Bosses and Their Prey

◆

Why does mobbing happen in a civilized society and in organizations that profess to value human resources?

The mobbing phenomenon is too complex to just blame it on one cause, for example, the bully boss. We suggest it comes about through the interaction of five elements that all play their part, relate to each other, and reinforce each other. They constitute a system. The parts are: The psychology and the circumstances of the mobbers; the organizational culture and structure; the psychology, personality, and circumstances of the mobbee; a triggering event, a conflict, and factors outside of the organization, i.e., values and norms in the U.S. culture. In understanding all these parts and their interrelation, we may be better equipped at finding solutions. Our exploration draws on different disciplines, such as psychology and sociology, anthropology and biology, as well as management theory.

THE PSYCHOLOGY AND
CIRCUMSTANCES OF THE MOBBERS

There is no empirical research dealing with the psychology of the mobbers. Yet, we suggest that the mobber's actions derive from his/her inability to value life and difference, from pretense and dishonesty, from an inflated sense of self, i.e., from a need for self-aggrandizement. The personality of the mobber has been described with such traits as excessively controlling, cowardly, neurotic, and power hungry. Many of his or her actions may be driven by jealousy and envy derived from feelings of insecurity and fear. Mobbing occurs because people, sometimes without even realizing their harmful ways, act in an evil manner.

Unequivocally, we believe that the actions and the psychology of the mobbers are central in attempting to understand mobbing reasons. Leymann maintains that people resort to mobbing to cover up their own deficiencies. Their fear and insecurity about their own reputation or position compel them to denigrate someone else.[1] He sees mainly four reasons why individuals would engage in mobbing behaviors.

1. **To force someone to adapt to a group norm.** "If they don't adapt, they have to go," would be the reasoning of someone driven by these motives. Belief that the group can only be cohesive and strong if a certain uniformity exists.

2. **To revel in animosity.** People engage in mobbing to "eliminate" those they do not like. It does not really matter where they are in the organizational hierarchy: Superiors, co-workers, or subordinates alike, when driven by personal dislikes, not prejudices, can initiate the process.

3. **To gain pleasure, out of boredom.** Sadistically motivated mobbers derive pleasure from the torment they inflict. Their primary intent might not necessarily be to get rid of the person.

4. **To reinforce prejudices.** People use mobbing behaviors because they dislike or hate people who happen to belong to a certain social, racial, or ethnic group. In the U.S. context, this is clearly discrimination, and the civil rights laws protect anybody who may be mobbed based on discrimination.[2]

Evil Personality

In his book, *People of the Lie*, psychiatrist M. Scott Peck espouses a theory of the evil personality. Peck contends that evil "is that force, residing either inside or outside of human beings, that seeks to kill life or liveliness."[3] Evil people use "power to destroy the spiritual growth of others for the purpose of defending and preserving the integrity of their own sick selves. In short, it is scapegoating."[4]

In Peck's words: "Because in their hearts they consider themselves above reproach, they must lash out at anyone who does reproach them. They sacrifice others to preserve their self-image of perfection."[5]

Divine Right

In *Brutal Bosses and Their Prey*, Hornstein talks about the "divine right" of bosses who, because they work in an organizational hierarchy, consider it their prerogative to exercise their power as they please. Whoever reports to them is seen as automatically inferior.[6] All these behaviors may be accentuated in situations of stress and demand of high performance.

Additionally, people aspiring to high positions are often power hungry. They are not leaders—they are *quasi* leaders. Abuse comes from feeling weak and worthless and using the power of their role to compensate.[7]

Luis: *The senior vice president had worked for major industries most of his career before coming to us. I really respected him at first—he was fired by his organization and I hired him the next day. I supported him implicitly all of*

59

*these years. I see now that what he did within our
organization, to one of our managers and ultimately to
me, was something he had a lot of practice doing.
Apparently, he'd done it many times before.*

Or in Howard's words: *There was this evaluation where they
said, "You are more loyal to the board than you are to
the three men in this room." They were just out to
provoke me. They just set me up to look insubordinate.
They have this inferiority complex. The only thing
they've got is power, and they were using that power
over me. They were going to smash me like a bug, like a
fly, and they were waiting for an opportunity to do it.*

Threatened Egotism, Inflated Self-Appraisal

Howard's insight fits Roy F. Baumeister and his colleagues' theory.
They say "what drives people to commit violent and oppressive
actions" may come from *threatened egotism,* particularly when it
consists of favorable *self-appraisals* that may be *inflated* or *ill-founded*
and that are confronted with an external evaluation that disputes
them." The explanation is that "anger is being directed outward as a
way of avoiding a downward revision of the self-concept."[8]

Their explanation of the threatened self-image would fit the
circumstances of many incidences experienced by us and our interview partners. In several of our cases it appears that, particularly in
the case of the "new boss" situation, s/he may have felt threatened by
an outstanding reputation of an employee reporting directly to him
or by "older" experienced staff that could upstage his or her glory.

Instead of feeling proud of having someone of exceptional
qualities on board, they feel threatened.

Howard: *I wanted to support the change. I asked him: Am I
on your team? He said "Yes," very clearly. But I had a
feeling he was lying.*

Neil: *They play on loyalty. They say, "I want you to stick
around, be part of the team." They cover their butts,
get their feet on the ground, but then . . .*

*I am a very loyal person, but loyalty is a two-way
street. When loyalty ceases on that other side, my
loyalty stops. A lot of people keep on being loyal.
You expect me to give, and you don't give? I'll dust
off my resume.*

Diana: *Eventually, I think most were sickened by this
behavior. But initially they thought it was the CEO's
style and it would change after some victims were out
of the organization. Hopefully, everything would go
back to normal. After a calm period, though, he started
in on others.*

*I have never seen anyone look the way he did when he
was screaming or demeaning staff. I will always believe
his abusive tactics were sadistic and that he received
some sort of sexual gratification from them.*

Peck in his analysis of evil presents the thesis that "evil can be
defined as a specific form of mental illness."[9] However, who can con-
ceive of leaders in companies having a mental illness? And yet, it
may happen for two reasons. For one, carefully selected CEO's
or other staff that have these traits might conceal them well. And,
as Hornstein contends, they might actually have been selected
for that very reputation to have an iron hand at streamlining, i.e.,
mobbing people in a company. "Chainsaw Al" Dunlap, downsizing
consultant/CEO, was a case in point.[10]

Narcissistic Personality

In their book *Work Abuse*, Judith Wyatt and Chauncey Hare go so
far as saying:

> Clinically speaking, any socially dysfunctional person who feels entitled to use power to control others he is afraid of, who lives in pretentious fantasy rather than reality, and who consistently views himself as superior to his fellow human beings and craves being told so, has a mental disorder called narcissistic personality disorder (according to the American Psychiatric Association's diagnostic manual).[11]

People generally do not harass an individual based on who s/he is, but rather based upon what that individual represents to them. What may seem to be petty office politics, is, in Marilyn Moats Kennedy's words, office warfare.[12] Envy, jealousy, aspirations, and being challenged are reasons individuals mob. Co-workers might resent someone for performing better, for looking better, for being more liked. They fear others' competence. When co-workers or subordinates are challenged by a higher performing co-worker, they might resent this and, as a consequence, start to mob. Their performance can now be judged against someone else's who is doing better, is smarter, is more productive. Subordinates or co-workers who initiate a mobbing can be guided by a wish to attain that person's job. They want to "climb the ladder" not based on their performance, but by an attempt to eliminate those who might be in their way.

> When Joan was mobbed by a former colleague who
> became her boss, she said to him: *You told me the
> first time I met you that you wanted my job. I believe
> that you have gone out of your way to look for any and
> every opportunity to embarrass me professionally and to
> discredit me.*

To explain this behavior, Brodsky refers to biology and anthropology and says in his *The Harassed Worker*,

> Competition is ubiquitous in all social, ethnic, and racial groups. There is a constant process of testing, of matching of self against others in order to establish one's place in the hierarchy . . .

> Harassment is a mechanism for achieving exclusion and protection of privilege in situations where there are no formal mechanisms available . . .
>
> Whether it occurs among nations or among individuals at the highest or lowest socioeconomic and political levels, harassment seems to be a social instinct. In the same way that a small dog of a species with instinctive bird-hunting abilities, or an animal trained to hunt rodents, goes through the entire ritual even though there are no birds or no rodents around, human beings fall easily into harassment behavior even when there seems no rational objective.[13]

The theory that explains individual and group mobbing behaviors as a genetic remnant from times past, i.e., a mechanism that served groups well that had to fend off an enemy or that were out to hunt, cannot scientifically be discarded. However, it is equally valid that culture, societal values, and education can change and influence genetic make-up.

Reverting to psychology, we cannot end this section without asking "Why, then, do people—bosses, co-workers or subordinates—engage in mobbing behaviors on the job?"

We suggest that in some cases the mobbers themselves may have been victims of childhood traumas, of horrific "parenting", of influences in their lives with which they were not able to come to terms. Wyatt and Hare's book, *Work Abuse*, is based on the theory that abusers and scapegoaters are acting out on the job—in their new family—because of how they have internalized and dealt with feelings of shame and fear in their childhood. These mechanisms are unconscious but may, in conducive circumstances, impact their adult behaviors powerfully.[14]

Why do Mobbers Seldom Come Alone?

To find an answer to this question, theories derived from social psychology and group dynamics are helpful. Persons who have a weakened sense of self feel more secure in a group in which they find support. They often "vulture", lacking the courage to listen to their conscience. They find their identity by associating with someone believed stronger, respected, idolized.

> I think what happens, said Dr. K. Westhues, is that beyond some threshhold, mob psychology takes over, like when a pack of dogs attacks. *The only relevant reality at that point, far beyond any personality characteristics of either the mobbee or the leading mobster, is the pack, the herd, a number of individuals having surrendered their selves to something bigger.*[15]

The need to be led and be part of a group might be reinforced by the fear of being excluded if they are different, stand out, or stand up. It often is the case as well that co-workers join the mobbing process out of intimidation or fear of personal repercussions. If they do not join in, they themselves might be in jeopardy.

> Diana: *One person had the strength to support me. He would give me a knowing glance. It was minor, but it gave me a great deal of strength. I always told him that he was my Schindler, I am forever grateful for that.*

Why Does the Mobbing Continue Even After a Resignation or Expulsion?

Mobbing sometimes continues after individuals have left the organization. Although this can rarely be proven, slandering continues. Some interview partners even reported that they have been personally hounded months after they had left the organization.

> Steven: *I was at the college for eight years where stabbing in one's back was pretty much the accepted way of life. It was not something that was provoked by a change in the CEO. It was built into the culture. There are probably half a dozen or a dozen names that I could mention. It happened to people who represented perceived threats to the established culture.*

I had a particularly vicious situation. I had another job which was 99% sure at another college. Somebody called the new school with charges that were untrue. The bottom line was, I did not get the job and there were really devastating effects there for a while.

This ongoing mobbing, even after individuals are no longer connected with the organization, seems to justify the mobbers previous behavior and upholds the organization's decision. They try to defend themselves by continuing to destroy the victim's reputation and by preserving the myth of the "difficult" employee.

We offered a number of possible explanations for the mobbers' evil conduct and the circumstances that drive them to engage in it. Perhaps by better understanding their motives, we might muster pity, compassion, or even forgiveness? Some of us might. Would that understanding help some mobbees overcome their suffering and humiliation? For some it might.

THE ORGANIZATIONAL CULTURE AND STRUCTURE

Mobbing occurs in all kinds of workplaces and in all types of organizations. However, the Scandinavian research tells us that in the nonprofit sector as well as in the education and health care industry, mobbing is more prevalent than in larger companies. Smaller nonprofit organizations may be more often led by persons poorly versed in management. This, plus the perpetual financial pressures, may be causes for higher mobbing incidents. Luis mentioned yet another reason:

Luis: *I think, generally speaking, those in nonprofit organizations are the kind of people whose personalities allow them to be more vulnerable. This is what got them into the business of serving people in the first place. I don't think I ever could have been as effective in my roles if I didn't have that vulnerability. I just had to take that risk. It is my belief that the CEO of a nonprofit has one role and that is to empower everyone else. And if you have the right people, it's going to work. Most of the time it does. It doesn't when you sanction someone who isn't trustworthy. And that's the risk.*

For-profit organizations with adequate financial resources are more likely to have training departments in line with modern management techniques and profit becomes a measure of performance. Earlier we mentioned that mobbing can only persist as long as it is allowed to persist. Organizational leadership and effective grievance procedures would help to prevent mobbing misconduct, spot it early in the process, and do something about it. Examples of such procedures are presented in Chapters 6 and 7.

In the following paragraphs we will point to several organizational factors that might contribute to the mobbing occurrence and its persistence.

Bad Management

In 1976, Brodsky identified three ultimate, real, or rationalized purposes of harassment: to discipline, to increase productivity, or to condition reflexes (as in the military services).[16] Today this would be considered unacceptable management. Other elements of what we consider bad management are:

- Excessive bottom-line orientation at the expense of human resources.
- Highly hierarchical structures.
- No open door policy.
- Poor communication channels.
- Poor conflict-solving abilities and no or ineffective conflict management or grievance procedures in place.
- Weak leadership.
- Pervasive scapegoat mentality.
- Little or no team work.
- No or ineffective diversity education.

Business and many organizations should place a high value on efficiency, cost-cutting, and being better than the competition. These goals are important for successful business and a sound economy. But does bottom-line thinking too often override the ethical principle that human resources are a company's most important asset? And, to value employees in any organization, it is indispensable that empowerment should be pervasive. This is good leadership. Empowerment is manifested in good and open communication, participation in decision-making, conflict resolution, respecting and valuing diversity, especially in ideas, in team-work, and allowing a high degree of autonomy and control.

Stress-Intensive Workplace

In a perpetually high-stress environment, where the pressure to produce is constantly high, people can be mobbed at every level if they can't keep up with the demands made on them. Supervisors may mob under the pressure exerted on them by higher management; subordinates may participate in upward mobbing as they rebel against the person believed to be responsible for their stress.

Monotony

Not only does high work stress contribute to mobbing, but in a workplace that does not provide challenges and is relentlessly repetitive, boredom becomes another possible cause for mobbing to add excitement.[17]

Disbelief or Denial by Managers

Mobbing can be perpetuated because of disbelief that the practice exists by those in charge at a higher level. They do not relate to the mobbing phenomenon because it has not been recognized as yet as a widespread workplace problem. They simply do not know how to deal with it. Remember Robert? He endured mobbing behaviors from his supervisor for five years, went up the hierarchical ladder to alert highest management, and got the director's response: "I cannot believe this is happening." And then nothing was ever done.

A new CEO may be able to destroy well-respected employees with a board's approval. Boards usually trust their chosen leader at the expense of the lower-ranked mobbed individuals. Letting go of "difficult" employees seems less of a loss than challenging the new CEO.

Unethical Activities

When unethical activities, such as endangering employees, clients, or the environment, or conducting shady financial transactions are being exposed by employees, they may be mobbed for whistle-blowing.

Rather than openly and truthfully dealing with the problem, a company fears primarily for its reputation and the short-term bottom line and less for the harm it might inflict. Instead of tackling the situation head-on, management prefers to hush any potential difficulty, to scapegoat and to silence a person.

> John: *When I started working at this institution to be the dental provider for mentally retarded persons, I thought my job was to provide dentistry. As it turned out, the position was primarily a front, so that the institution could continue to get Federal funds for health care.*
>
> *Officially, I was the only licensed person and the only one qualified to provide care and supervise the assistants. In reality, the institution had set up a sham situation in which a person with a B.A. in social work was head of the dental department. It was a criminal institution before I ever got there.*

John's reports addressed to his superiors were ignored and his job was eventually eliminated.

Flat Organizations

In flat organizations, highly ambitious people who want and need promotions and or titles for their self-image, or because of financial goals, often resort to techniques that hamper the well being of others, such as mobbing, to further their own chances for advancement.

Downsizing, Restructuring, Mergers

Downsizing, restructuring, and merging are normal managerial decisions in the life of any organization. These practices may make perfect business sense and often cannot be avoided. But they may entail elimination of positions. If this is not done thoughtfully, mobbing may occur. In a competitive work environment, employees fearing for their jobs might fight for their positions. Rather than being eliminated themselves, they begin to mob others.

> Ron: *This was no coincidence. The time was convenient. I cannot prove it, I am imputing their motives. I think it was a strategy. They decided to fire me for cause when the last project was done.*

What we want to stress here is that mobbing is preventable by preparing people early on for any impending changes, by helping them to find other positions, and by offering severance packages to ease any transition.

> Judy: *My impression is that it is not uncommon for a new CEO to want to surround himself with his own people who tell him what he wants to hear. But I maintain that if this is the case, and you want people out of there, then use a humane way to do it. Tell people, "You know you do not fit into this plan. Do your best, but find something else within the next three-to-six months. Or take six months severance pay and we will help you with some outplacement." There is a decent way to do it.*
>
> *Do unto others as you wish it done unto you. It is a matter of values. It all comes down to values.*

PERSONALITY, PSYCHOLOGY AND
CIRCUMSTANCES OF THE MOBBEE

Can a case be made for personality traits that would be conducive to being mobbed? Can mobbees be held responsible for what happens to them? Researchers debate the question whether there is anything in a person's background, behavior, attitude, character, or circumstance that predisposes them to become mobbees. There is no evidence for this in the mobbing literature. According to Leymann, no case can be made for a personality issue as there is no research determining what individuals were like prior to being mobbed.[18]

Yet, we found that the people we interviewed were exceptional individuals. They demonstrated throughout their professional careers many positive qualities: intelligence, competence, creativity, integrity, accomplishment, and dedication. They were mostly people who Daniel Goleman would consider *emotionally intelligent*: in general, they have learned to work things out, they examine their own behaviors and they correct them when they see they have made a mistake.[19]

> Howard: *Before I lived through this, I always thought that when it happened to others, there was a reason. You were a jerk, you provoked it, you must have done something, you should have backed up at some point, you should have found out from them what it was they wanted. Basically, I've always believed you are responsible for what happens to you. That is why I struggle so much with this. I want to analyze it.*
>
> *I tried so hard to keep my job. I knew it was on the line when the new CEO came. If I would have started to look for another job, it would have been a sign of disloyalty. And that would have pushed me out the door faster.*

Dr. Kenneth Westhues, who wrote *Eliminating Professors* found in his study that "the professors who were ganged up on tend to be trusting, naive, politically inept, high achievers. In many cases they are indeed partially responsible for what happens to them, in the same way as Socrates was. They tend to be principled sorts of individuals, 'innerdirected' as opposed to 'otherdirected.' They are not go-with-the flow sorts of people."[20]

What we learned from our interview partners, however, is that people react quite differently to similar mobbing conduct and that they are differently affected by the syndrome. Those who successfully overcome the mobbing resort to their own strength and inner resources and develop survival strategies.

Why Me?

We seem to face a dilemma. Anybody can become a victim, and yet it seems that some people are picked out because of certain characteristics.

Wyatt and Hare believe in theories of childhood patterning.[21] They maintain that how a person learned survival skills and developed their own coping mechanisms as a child, how they learned to deal with shame and abuse in their developmental years will influence how they will manage to stand up to an abusive situation at work, or, as we said earlier, become abusers themselves. Similar thinking guided Neil Crawford, a psychotherapist, who wrote the chapter "The Psychology of the Bullied" in Andrea Adam's *Bullying at Work*.[22]

Individuals can be victimized no matter who they are, how old, devoted, loyal, creative, experienced, organized, responsible, how much initiative they demonstrate, or how much a team-player they are. Our interview partners, and this they all had in common, seemed to have a high degree of loyalty towards their organizations and were highly identified with their work or by their work. We suggest that particularly creative individuals may more often be subjected to mobbing, because they promote new ideas which may challenge others. Often mobbees are selected because they constitute a threat to a higher-positioned person.

Judy: *No matter who you are, everything goes back to this intolerance of anybody who is different, or has a different style, rather than to appreciate everybody's strengths. If you work harder and you try to excel, you*

71

*put pressure on them. If you work long hours, they
assume you do not work smart. If you are single, you
are more vulnerable.*

One answer to the question "Can a case be made for a person's own responsibility of becoming a mobbing target?" is given by Dr. Kenneth Westhues. He writes: "One can make a typology of ways of being different. Some of them—skin colour, sex, physical appearance, foreign accent, the manners of a class higher or lower than workmates, belonging to a pariah people like Jews, Gypsies, Indians—are qualities a person can't do much about. Other ways of being different—the ratebuster, whistle-blower, champion of the underdog, the person who asks too many questions—are, to some extent, under the prospective mobbing target's control."[23] And it is these people who are so desperately needed.

The Dynamics of the Interaction

Because the conflict over procedures or tasks, personalities or values, and unethical behaviors, remains unresolved, it escalates. Attempts to find a solution are barred by unwillingness of the other person or of the organization. The course of events forces some into subjugation and depression, and others into action that runs against the organization's interests. This may have a devastating effect on their confidence. They feel vulnerable, disempowered, confused, and weak.

This in turn might bring out behaviors in them that now give rise to complaints by their superiors or co-workers. As others now begin to display mobbing behaviors, the victim is pushed even further into a defensive behavior. The more the mobbee reacts in this way, the more the mobbers have a reason to intensify their behavior, sometimes to the point of causing the mobbee to become paranoid or dysfunctional. This spiral can then lead to the expulsion phase in the mobbing process—often under the accusation of mental illness.

There is often very little, or perhaps nothing, that the mobbee can do to change these dynamics. And the mobbers are far from wanting to change their behavior. Companies with effective conflict management procedures can avoid this course of events.

Coping and Outcome Determined by Beliefs

How well persons cope with seemingly unresolvable conflicts, personal attacks, and victimization is determined by their character and their personality, their life experience and above all, by their beliefs.

There are mobbees who are in denial of what is happening to them. But the persistent assaults begin to affect their mental and physical health. They change. They cannot function normally. Some are less productive, less creative. As they internalize their feelings, they become depressed, obsessive, irritable, or aggressive. Either way, their hurt affects their health.

Some have a higher tolerance level than others and are better able to shield themselves from the assaults. They use many of the survival tactics described in Chapter 4 and may survive longer, irrespective of the circumstances. Robert, for example, withstood a boss for five years who undermined him continuously. He was able to withstand the ordeal, largely based on his strong religious beliefs:

> Robert: *At first it made me very obstinate. I thought of things to do, even to take it to higher authorities, and initiate formal discrimination procedures, and get the federal government involved. I started documenting everything that was going on. I still have the documentation. But it looked like a hopeless case. I prayed a lot. The Lord told me what to do about it. To be at peace with it. I did a lot of praying and fasting. I stayed because there were a lot of people there who were dependent on me.*

Some will stand up earlier and plan to escape. Others may wish to escape; however, circumstances prevent them from doing so.

Individuals might be especially vulnerable at the time of the mobbing because of other unsettling matters in their lives—relationship issues, concerns about children, parents, or illness, deaths of loved ones, and financial difficulties. In such circumstances, it often is overwhelming to also take on the task of a job search combined with possible resettlement.

More often than not, other constraints make it difficult to quit and change jobs. Victims depend on their job for financial reasons, or because of the particular location of the job, or because they believe their age may preclude another job search. Thus they attempt to withstand the mobbing.

Knowing how harmful the mobbing cycle can become, we would advise them to nevertheless start looking for other jobs as quickly as they can, and to seek mental health care by professionals who really understand workplace abuse. This understanding still seems to be quite rare. We also refer to Wyatt and Hare's book *Work Abuse*, where victims can find helpful advice on how to empower themselves to withstand the situation if they decide they have no other choice but to "tough-it-out" a bit longer.

Another explanation why individuals sometimes endure being victimized without standing up comes from Susan's insight. A tour guide for 16 years and director of a multi-lingual service, she was stripped of her responsibility and offered a lower ranking job. Although it was a humiliating experience, she expressed that she was burned out, and she tried to view her demotion in a positive light.

> Susan: *I was not suffering all the time. I kept my ego out of the bargain as long as I could. I have a very practical side. To tell you the truth, I was not devastated. I was kind of relieved, because I was sick and tired of dealing with the bullshit in the position that I was in. The main thing that bothered me was, I now had to share an office with someone. I had no privacy whatsoever, and the office was small and uncomfortable. That bothered me and I was bored. When you are used to running a whole department…that was hard.*

In some cases, a demotion that puts less stress on the individual might actually be a welcome change. Nevertheless, some suffering cannot be denied:

> Susan: *I was tired all the time. All the time. A form of depression. I did not exercise anymore. I did not do things for myself. At home I did nothing. I watched a lot of television. I was hiding. I was in constant hiding.*

In conclusion, we want to stress that even if we could make a case that certain dispositions of the mobbee might contribute to the mobbing syndrome, they cannot, under any circumstance, be accepted as an excuse for the syndrome to occur.

THE TRIGGERING EVENT BECOMES A CONFLICT

A disagreement or a conflict sets the mobbing cycle into motion. In most cases, however, that very event is virtually irrelevant. It does not matter what the cause of the conflict is, whether it is a disagreement over a work procedure, a lack of recognition, incivility, harassment, a new boss or co-worker, or a clash of personalities or values. The event becomes an excuse to set the mobbing into motion.

What matters is that the cause of the conflict is not addressed openly and truthfully and the issues are not really dealt with. Thus the conflict lingers on and may escalate, because the individual has no way of addressing the issue with anyone in the organization. This compounds the original conflict.

An organizational culture that suppresses conflict, or a supervisor who does not want to deal with a conflict in a cooperative manner, constitutes a prime reason for setting the mobbing cycle into motion. Because unresolved conflicts are a crucial element in triggering and intensifying the mobbing process, we deal with conflict in detail in Chapter 7.

FACTORS OUTSIDE OF THE ORGANIZATION VALUES AND NORMS IN THE U.S. CULTURE

The values and norms of a society, its economic structure and philosophy influence the culture of an organization. For example, success only measured in economic terms or glorified violence may negatively influence behaviors of people working in companies.

Disposable Workers

Sharpened economic competition and strictly bottom-line thinking encourages a philosophy that sees workers as expendable. The term *workforce* is so common that few think about the fact that it is made up of individual human beings. Even the term *human resources* sounds more like an euphemism: humans are seen as resources much like money or technology—and not as creative human beings accomplishing a task for their own fulfillment.

Increasingly, part-time work, flexibility, and the independence of consultants adds opportunities and fulfills individual and organizational needs. However, there is a real downside to this societal trend as well. As David Yamada says, "Such arrangements discourage the creation of positive interpersonal bonds that can be forged in traditional long-term employment settings. Instead, workers are depersonalized and deemed disposable. In such a setting, they are more likely to be treated in an emotionally abusive manner." [24]

"Emotional Labor"

Paradoxically, our service-oriented society seems to fuel the mobbing syndrome as well. Quoting Amy S. Wharton, Yamada says, "Because service-sector work is so dependent on personal interaction, it becomes a form of "emotional labor" in which the psychological consequences of work, both positive and negative, are easily exacerbated, especially in comparison to the more mundane yet steady working conditions of a manufacturing plant." [25]

◆

The table to the right summarizes some typical traits of the U.S. culture that, if taken to the extreme, may lead to mobbing behaviors.

On the other hand, the U.S. culture can also be identified with such values as caring for others, helping, assisting, cooperating, supporting, and respecting diversity. Applied to successful management, these values become empowerment, team-work, conflict management, inclusion, and participation. Where cooperation is the norm, the work environment can be productive and supportive— and free of mobbing.

Typical Traits in American Culture	Exaggerated Manifestations May Lead to Mobbing
Competitiveness.	Competition can lead to ruthlessness. Where this abounds, mobbing will be prevalent.
Success-oriented. Often measured in dollars.	May lead to "climbing the ladder" through mobbing.
Individualistic. Personal goals supersede other's goals. It also means that individuals can choose how to live their lives and that it is up to them to achieve success.	Individualism can also mean: You alone are responsible for your behavior. It is your choice to go if you don't like it here.
Direct and practical.	Practical approaches to problems can also mean sacrificing individuals for bottom-line thinking.
Efficient.	Very efficient procedures do not always go together with participatory structures and open communication.
Hard-working.	Being too dedicated may constitute a threat to others.
Freedom-loving. Antagonistic to being controlled.	Not wanting to be controlled can also mean: I can do as I please. Freedom of choice can also mean: If you don't like it here, go somewhere else.
Innovative.	Suggesting or creating changes too often creates unrest.
Direct interaction.	Directness can become personal attacks.
Relationships often not deep or long-lasting.	The workforce is a means to an end.

Chapter 2 Endnotes

1. Leymann, 1993:28.

2. Leymann, 1993:35.

3. Peck, 1998:43.

4. Peck, 1998:119.

5. Peck, 1998:73.

6. Hornstein, 1996:40.

7. Wyatt and Hare, 1988:102.

8. Baumeister et al., 1996:5.

9. Al Dunlap made millions advising companies to fire people. He has fired tens of thousands, only to help others prosper. *Time Magazine*, March 16, 1998:44.

10. Peck, 1998:67.

11. Wyatt and Hare, 1998:100, 101.

12. Marilyn Moats Kennedy, *Office Warfare*.

13. Brodsky, 1976:4.

14. Wyatt and Hare, 1998:56 ff.

15. Personal communication, March 13, 1999. Dr. K. Westhues is the author of *Eliminating Professors*.

16. Brodsky, 1976:2.

17. Schueppach, Torre, 1996:94, 95.

18. Reference: Personal communication and Leymann, 1995.

19. Daniel Goleman, 1995, and 1998.

20. Personal communication, March 2, 1999.

21. Wyatt and Hare, 1998.

22. Andrea Adams with Neil Crawford, 1992.

23. Personal Communication, March 2, 1999.

24. Yamada, David. The Phenomenon of "Workplace Bullying" and the Need for Status-blind Hostile Environment Protection. *Georgetown Law Journal*, Vol. 8, Nr. 3, 2002, p. 491.

25. Yamada, David. The Phenomenon of "Workplace Bullying" and the Need for Status-blind Hostile Environment Protection. *Georgetown Law Journal*, Vol. 8, Nr. 3, 2002, p. 487.

THREE

How Mobbing Affects You

You can kill a person only once, but when you humiliate him, you kill him many times over.

—The Talmud

Howard: *It is tremendously traumatic, what has happened to me. It is my whole life, my whole career that these guys were able to throw out. But it is happening every day, everywhere, to a lot of people.*

Diana: *I'll never forget them getting me to the point where I should have been crawling in there every day. Yet every morning I managed to get the strength to go to work with dignity. I am very proud of that.*

◆

In this chapter we address the person living through the mobbing experience. We focus on the feelings you may go through, on the impact mobbing may have on you, and why it can affect you and your health.

A STRONG COMMITMENT TO THE JOB

Why does mobbing affect you so deeply? One of the key factors we found is that many mobbing victims love their work. They are identified strongly with what they do. They feel a great commitment to their work and derive purpose and pleasure from it. Mobbing violates a person's professional integrity and self-image. Self-doubt abounds.

People who do not have a strong commitment to their work often view a job more as a necessary means to earn a livelihood. It does not serve as fulfillment, an opportunity to be challenged and to grow. In a mobbing, these people may more easily turn their backs on the organization and go some place else. They leave without great remorse. "I'm out of here. I hope I never see this place again!"

But employees who are committed to their work are often very loyal. They believe in the goals of the organization. They care about the organization's reputation. They keep quiet, are ambivalent about taking action and may not readily seek assistance, inside or outside the organization. They suffer for a longer period. Rarely do such individuals reveal their personal agony. And often they do not understand the complex reality of their situation.

Why is it that people turn against you?

Feeling Confused, Isolated and Paranoid

Howard: *I was kind of paranoid. How are they going to get me? How are they going to set me up? Everyone is after me! Everything has changed. My friends, all the people that I worked with, my closest people in my office, all of a sudden they would not talk to me.*

You may feel confused and betrayed. Why is it that people turn against you?

Diana: *One minute I totally accepted that nobody would come forward and support me, but the next minute I thought, "How can all these people just go along with this?" That to me was incredible and it was one of the hardest things. Yet, I would think, "I can't blame these people. I know they have to go along with this for their own survival, so they can collect their paychecks."*

There may be a feeling of constant danger.

Joan: *During the experience, I dreamed two subordinates came to my home and said, "We are really sorry that we have to do this, but we have to watch out for ourselves and our own families." Then they murdered me. I woke up feeling very frightened.*

You may isolate yourself. The emotions of embarrassment, fear, shame, anger, guilt, disgrace, anxiety, and feelings of incompetence may pervade.

Joan: *I still feel isolated. I have never come completely out of it. I still feel embarrassed. Sometimes I feel like I do not want to deal with people ever again. Like Grizzly Adams, go to the mountains, in some cabin. When you feel so terribly rejected, you begin to reject others before they have the opportunity to reject you. I thought most people were good. Now I think 2% are good.*

83

Diana: *I was so embarrassed. I just wanted to hide. It is four years later and I'm still embarrassed.*

Our interview partners, without exception, experienced severe anxiety during the mobbing and following their expulsion from the workplace. These feelings were pervasive enough to affect all aspects of their lives.

Judy: *They are telling you something. But you are feeling something else. And then you begin to think, "Am I nuts? Am I just imagining this? Am I paranoid?" Then pretty soon it is so obvious, you can't help but identify it.*

What happens most often is that the victims feel alone. They cannot believe what is happening to them. It is both difficult to express, and difficult for others to understand. "Just move on," is the advice often given.

Most of all, victims report feeling a total loss of self-esteem. They do not recognize themselves anymore. They report terrible, debilitating fear of being physically hurt, being emotionally hurt, or losing control.

Jack: *The paranoia was always there because from the time that he told me about what was coming, I knew that everything that I said and did was going to be questioned, evaluated, and looked at more severely than anyone else. I'm certain that the amount of time it took me to do things at that point was a lot longer, because everything that I said and did I thought through so many times. It took longer because I evaluated and re-evaluated everything.*

Diana: *While I was going through all this, I can remember thinking, "I have to stay focused, I have to make sure that I do not do any crazy things." I was so afraid that I would forget to put on my underpants and they would find out. I have never, in all my life, ever thought such crazy things in such a serious way.*

When a person is stripped of responsibility, identity, personality, and reputation, the person feels exposed, naked, extremely vulnerable. Diana's seemingly peculiar fear expresses this state of mind.

Diana: *It was like being stripped naked to the core. I thought, "I must maintain my composure, my dignity, but inside ..."*

For some, mobbing is a violation of the soul.

"DIFFICULT" BECOMES RE-VICTIMIZATION

The persistent emotional assaults affect the person's health, outlook, and state of mind. The repetitive attacks change normal reasoning and ways of communicating. Victims become defensive, attempting to make sense of what seems senseless. Their fear, and their feeling of betrayal impacts their behavior and self-control. They stop trusting.

When the victims finally decide to seek assistance, their functioning, physical health, and/or psychological condition has been so affected by the mobbing that it causes the person to appear to be a "difficult case" even to those who are approached for support. *Now the victims become the accused and responsibility for the mobbing is laid on them.*[1]

PERSISTENT ATTACKS

> *The normal pressures of the job, coupled with the added psychological trauma of the mobbing experience, often do not allow the individual to recover sufficiently between the attacks.*

Sean attempted to take some long weekends off, for which he had accumulated time and which had been approved according to company policy. He was confronted by a supervisor involved in the mobbing who stated that he seemed to be "taking a lot of time off."

A few days of distance can help you experience temporary relief and you may gain some strength. You may want to believe that things have changed when you get back. But be prepared that you may, once again, be subjected to mobbing. Though helpful and often necessary, frequent sick leaves will necessarily be held against you. You are trapped.

> Carol: *I am sorry that I worked with him as long as I did because in some ways, he "wrecked" me. You really do question yourself. You wonder if you are any good, you wonder if you can do it. You just kind of get wrecked He undermined my self confidence. And now I am more jaded than I used to be. Then I say to myself, there is no perfect world. There is no perfect world, so what do I want?*

To someone unaware of the gravity of mobbing, Carol's concerns sound "par for the course" in this world of work. This interview was nine months after Carol's experience and she was proud of moving on. But when we saw her earlier, in the midst of the mobbing experience, she was unbelievably thin, and had the look of someone being hunted. She was trying to look strong, but she was so frantic that we worried for her life.

HELP IS OUT OF REACH

Most of our interview partners had been in the workforce for at least fifteen years, many much longer, and were competent, capable, stable individuals used to dealing with the deadlines and work pressures that characterize many American workplaces. Yet, they were utterly startled and in disbelief of what was happening to them. Wherever they turned, help was out of reach.

The following is Diana's report of a conversation she had with the Director of Human Resources of her company:

> Diana: *He said, "Why don't you just get out?" And I said, "Why should I get out when I've built all of this and I haven't done anything wrong? I just don't understand the whole thing." He then said, "Don't you know everybody thinks you're crazy?" "Crazy?" I said, "Everybody thinks I'm crazy?" He said, "Yes, everybody thinks you're crazy."*

COMPOUNDING FACTORS

As mentioned earlier, individuals might be especially vulnerable when subjected to mobbing due to other matters causing stress in their lives. If people are centered and reasonably happy, they can cope with worries or distress in positive ways.

Several of our interview partners experienced, simultaneously with the mobbing, divorce or the severe disruption of significant relationships. Whether this would have happened regardless of the mobbing we cannot say. Perhaps a separation or a divorce had been in the making for some time, and the tensions and disruptions on the job precipitated the decision.

We can also assume that tensions at home might have an effect on how much at ease a person feels in the work environment. Relationship problems generally impact work performance negatively and thus may intensify the course of the mobbing. The loss of a significant relationship can compound the feeling of failure and contribute further to the sense of despair.

> Joan: *"My marriage created a lot of additional stress. I mentioned at work that I was getting a divorce. That was when the steamroller process began."*

Concerns of such magnitude in anyone's life cannot be well hidden. They affect one's outlook and behavior in one way or another.

It appears that the mobbers often use these stressful times to further their goal. Mobbers may use stress in a person's life as a smokescreen to question the victim's objectivity when he or she attempts to expose the mobbing activity. Now they find even more grounds to accuse the victim, to point out faults and "difficult" behavior.

DEGREES OF MOBBING AND THE EFFECTS ON YOUR HEALTH

Earlier we distinguished between three degrees of mobbing, based on how deeply an individual is injured by the mobbing experience.

The damage caused by the repeated emotional assaults is gradual and cumulative rather than singular and explosive. Since confusion and isolation are part of the mobbing experience, it may be difficult to recognize danger signals and to seek help before symptoms become severe and a potential illness more difficult to alleviate. Again, we advise you to seek professional help early.

Normal stress management techniques may be a temporary help for first degree mobbing, but are, in general, totally inadequate to address the continual and prolonged impact of the mobbing process.

The following physical and psychological symptoms are a summary of our interview partners' experiences combined with information from the mobbing and work abuse literature. You may experience other symptoms. Often, becoming physically ill may serve to hide the despair of the emotional assaults. *Physical illness seems easier to deal with than anguish and is often better understood by others.*

First Degree Mobbing

> Catherine: *I was terribly distraught. It affected me to the point that I had problems sleeping. I cried. I felt out of balance. It was like being sucked into a totally new environment. The atmosphere around you changes drastically, and then you don't know anymore how you fit in. It is like plants when they are neglected. They wilt.*

Experiencing humiliating behaviors from colleagues is confusing and causes distress. Individuals may feel angry and upset. Some may try to confront the people, others may just tolerate what is going on. They begin to dislike the work environment and may think about looking for employment elsewhere. Even though the person remains generally functional, symptoms, such as the following may occur:

- crying
- occasional sleep difficulties
- irritability
- lack of concentration

Relationships with family and friends are not affected. Generally, interventions that deal with stress reduction such as meditating, exercising, distraction, balancing activities such as the pursuit of a hobby, help as a temporary measure.

When the situation persists it can develop into second degree mobbing.

Second Degree Mobbing

Jack: *I have a pretty high tolerance for stress. Emotionally it was pretty bad. I felt as though there was a head hunt going on. I did not know how to handle it, nor what caused it. It was very disturbing. Maybe it was affecting me more than I realized. My wife later told me that she thought if I hadn't gotten out of there I would have had a heart attack. I didn't know I was showing any physical symptoms.*

People exposed to frequent mobbing activities over a longer time can have such symptoms as:

- high blood pressure
- persistent sleep difficulties
- gastro-intestinal problems

- concentration difficulties
- excessive weight gain or weight loss
- depression
- alcohol or drug abuse
- avoidance of the workplace (being late or absent more frequently, seeking more off-site work)
- uncharacteristic fearfulness (with no apparent reason developing a fear of flying, driving, or being alone)

Family and friends sense that something is wrong, but they are confused or might minimize the difficulty you experience at work. Your health problems begin to affect your work. Seeking medical and therapeutic help is indicated.

Judy said, recovering at home from what we believe was a second degree mobbing:

> It destroys you more than you know. I am scared to death to go back to work. I have this feeling I am not going to be successful anywhere. It damages you forever. I have no confidence. I really believe that now I am not as competent.

Third Degree Mobbing

Elizabeth: "For 17 years I gave my heart and energy to my job. Finally, the many years of abuse took its toll. When arriving at work one morning, I couldn't enter the building. I knew I couldn't face the abuse ever again. I went back to my car, and drove away. I never returned. It's been four years. I've had therapy, and even now as we talk about it, I am so agitated. So many months I felt like I was crippled. I knew I still had my legs, but I thought I couldn't walk. Then I felt like I was having a heart attack. I had several panic attacks and I thought I was dying."

In third degree mobbing, people are no longer able to perform. They go to work with dread, fear or disgust. They are so affected that they are unable to remain in the work environment. They are ill and their self-defense mechanisms have broken down. Extreme physical and/or psychological episodes occur such as:

- severe depression
- panic attacks
- heart attacks
- other severe illness
- accidents
- suicide attempts
- violence directed at third parties

These must be seen as severe warning signals to family and friends. Medical and psychological care is now imperative.

> Diana: *"After I left, I managed to do some freelance work,*
> *but I was totally wiped out. I had been so beaten down*
> *by the horrible experience. I knew there was something*
> *physically wrong. Earlier, I had said to my attorney,*
> *"I'm trying to remain calm throughout this because I*
> *don't want to end up with cancer." He would always*
> *assure me, "You are not going to end up with cancer."*
> *My brother had died of cancer at my age, and I knew*
> *that traumatic events sometimes trigger illness. I*

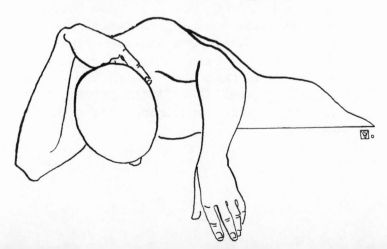

thought, "I will just rest, exercise, do all the things that make sense, and then pretty soon, I'll be strong again." But I got progressively worse. For 2 1/2 years after I lost my job, I went to doctors. I had intestinal problems all the time. My immune system was very low. Finally, after getting down to 100 pounds, I found a physician who discovered a precancerous mass. In a matter of months, I would have been dealing with cancer. I came so close to what I had feared would be the conclusion of this evil ordeal.

SYMPTOMS OF PROLONGED ANXIETY

Leymann cites eighteen symptoms connected with prolonged anxiety. These conditions, protracted over a period of time, may cause long-term physical complications and illness. Our interview partners mentioned many of these.

Muscular Tension Symptoms
Trembling, jumpy, shaky
Tense, aching or sore muscles
Restlessness
Unusual fatigue

Autonomic Nervous System Hyperactivity
Oxygen debt or a feeling of shortness of breath
Heart palpitations or rapid pulse
Sweating or cold wet hands
Dryness of the mouth
Dizziness or giddiness
Feeling sick, diarrhea, other gastro-intestinal difficulties
Feelings of suddenly being quite warm or cold
Frequent need to urinate
Difficulties in swallowing or "lump in the throat"

Tense Vigilance and Hypersensitivity
Agitated or "uptight"
Overreacting to unexpected external stimuli
Concentration difficulties or "completely blank mind"
Difficulties in falling asleep or uneasy sleep
Irritability

POST-TRAUMATIC STRESS DISORDER

Following the prolonged emotional assaults of mobbing, many victims may experience post-traumatic stress disorder (PTSD) similar to that experienced by combat soldiers, victims of torture or rape, or by persons after major disasters. This is what Leymann suggests, as do Wyatt and Hare in their book on work abuse.[2] The excessive threat and danger causes intense fear and helplessness manifested in the following symptoms.

* Continually reliving the event/flashbacks
* Hyperalertness, easily startled, edgy
* Fatalistic outlook on life
* General emotional numbing
* Persisting anxiety
* Nightmares
* Insomnia
* Poor concentration
* Uncontrolled acting out
* Attacks of intense anxiety or panic
* Feeling suicidal and/or homicidal

Because any reminder of the trauma generally provokes intense feelings of distress, people with PTSD typically avoid situations in any way similar to the traumatic experience. One of our interview partners could not enter an office environment without experiencing panic anxiety.[3]

Others experience an enduring personality change as a result of the workplace trauma, and become identified as a "difficult" person. This, more often than not, may lead to misinterpreting what has actually happened at the workplace: the change happened as a result–and not the cause–of workplace mobbing.[4]

Despair and rage may push some people to the extremes. They commit acts of violence–directed at themselves or at the mobbers and even at innocent people. Feeling hopeless and destroyed, some individuals may take their lives.

Howard: *I thought about suicide. We all have our baggage in our lives. And there is a certain amount of depression in aging. And then you go through something like this. You have to have an awful strong self esteem and an awful strong sense of security and guidance and spirituality. I used to think that I had that. But I also have been going through divorce. It has been a challenge to the end. I see why people commit suicide, why people jump off bridges, and I see why people can't put it together.*

Some may feel revengeful and direct their rage at the mobbers. Seeking revenge for their misery, they may "go postal."[5]

Joan: *I am a civilized person who detests violence. But, during this experience, I did say to my mother and a couple of close friends, "Now I know how those postal workers feel when they walk in and spray the entire workplace with bullets. Because I am that angry."*

◆

Chapter 3 Endnotes

1. See Leymann, 1996.

2. Leymann, 1993 and Wyatt and Hare, 1997:273.

3. Hoel et. al. (1999: 20) quote two researchers who suggest an important distinction that the PTSD definition "ought to distinguish between acute and enduring psychological stressors referring to the latter as Post-Traumatic Prolonged Duress (PTPD), and its possible implications for treatment."

4. PTSD has code number F 43.1 and enduring personality change after catastrophic experiences has code number F 62.0 as identified in the International Statistical Classification of Diseases and Related Health Problems, tenth revision (ICD -10.)

5. Not a year goes by in which we would not hear about "disgruntled" employees shooting co-workers and often also ending up killing themselves. Although the postal service seems to have a high incidence of workplace shootings, one has to take into consideration that they employ some 800,000 persons.

FOUR

How You Can Cope

Diana: *Some can rise to the occasion of the ugliness that they experience, perhaps because they have experienced more of it in their lives. They have developed a "thicker skin." Others have lived a sweeter life, are more sensitive, and are devastated by the experience.*

Thank God for the larger world. It is the only refuge for people burned by their employers.

—Kenneth Westhues
Eliminating Professors

———————————————— ♦ ————————————————

We have identified some of the more common physical and psychological symptoms of the mobbing syndrome as well as some extreme reactions. We now suggest ways that can help you overcome the experience, strengthen your self, and help you regain control to heal and move on. We discuss the significance of grieving, reactions to loss, steps you can take, options you have, and the importance of professional medical and legal help.

GRIEVING

Howard: *You are going through all the stages of grieving—the denial, the shock, and also the dysfunctional behavior.*

Diana: *I could not believe how much this felt like a death. I grieved when my mother and father died. But this grieving was for myself.*

Similar to experiencing a death of a loved one, mobbees experience a death of their own selves. In a like manner, they feel loss and they grieve. They also grieve the loss of "what might have been" if their work life had not taken this unexpected course.

Grieving is an inevitable and essential process, but our culture does not always allow for grieving. People are forever being advised to put situations behind them and to move on. We are locked in a place where grief is not honored either by the culture or by people around us. We are confused and embarrassed in the presence of the expression of strong emotions. This makes it difficult for people to work through their feelings, and even harder for those around them to comfortably and openly assist in the process.

If you are a victim of mobbing, give yourself time. Unexpressed and prolonged grief is one more form of stress that can impact your life.

Go through the grieving process. Do whatever feels right for you: remain silent in solitary mourning; engage in constructive activity; be more assertive and courageous. The void and empty feelings may be filled temporarily with busywork and "running-around" tasks. Eventually you will be able to focus and engage in reconstructing your life.

In general, men and women deal with their grief in different ways. Women may express their grief by talking, crying, and nurturing. As Tom Golden says, men may respond with anger, ritual, and action.

Many times, in working with men, I have found that while a man is expressing anger (and I mean really expressing it...loudly, with movement of the body, etc.), he suddenly will be moved to tears. It is almost as if touching on that profound and deep feeling of anger has brought him in touch with his other feelings.

This process is reversed with women. Many times a woman would be in tears, crying and crying. I might ask what her tears are about, and she often would state plainly and many times loudly, "I'm angry." [1]

REACTION VS. RESPONSE
DON'T ASSUME THAT YOU HAVE NO POWER

> Jack: *Oh, I went through a lot of the "I'm going to get back*
> *at you" stuff. That was counterproductive to what I*
> *needed to do which was to focus on this business now.*
> *I had planned to go on vacation anyway. While I was*
> *there, I had more time to think about where I needed to*
> *be putting my emphasis.*

We cannot control what comes into our lives. We can control whether we react or respond. Reaction is an emotional reflex. Response requires thought.

By assuming a victim mentality—feeling helpless, having no recourse, nobody will listen, there is nothing one can do—you become powerless. It is not easy to rise above this attitude when you feel overwhelmed and do not understand what is happening.

However, you have options. Mobbing does not take these away from you.

You have options, mobbing does not take these away from you.

OPTIONS

1. Analyze what is actually going on.

2. Attempt to work it out. In a nurturing environment with a process for conflict management, an employee should be able to find redress and a solution. However, when management is involved in the mobbing, the predicament of the situation preempts this option, and any attempt is futile.

3. Bear with it, protect yourself, and use survival strategies.

4. Plan an escape. Resign—with or without a new job. As disconcerting as that might be, seeking other employment is eminently more reasonable than sticking it out and having your emotional and physical well-being seriously affected by continuing to suffer indignation.

5. Fight with legal means while still on the job or soon after.

6. Disclose—whistle-blowing. Public whistle-blowing is courageous and may be important for your and others' sake, but weigh the consequences carefully. Do not blow the whistle without an exit strategy already in place.

7. Engage in positive action that uses your experience to help eliminate future mobbing situations.

Yet another option that some people consider is to take revenge through violence. Feeling depressed or angry, they direct violence at themselves or at the mobbers. *To avoid acting out on impulse, seek help quickly. Violence is not a rational choice.*

What is crucial is that you weigh all your options carefully and realistically in light of your specific situation and your assessment of the workplace culture. Early action and implementation of options is the best response.

NEIL'S STORY

Neil's story is one example of how one's attitude can function as a shield against the devastating effects of mobbing. A senior administrator, Neil had been on the job for three years when the mobbing started. The former director left for a different company, and an interim director took over.

Neil: *The first thing he did was tell me that he did not want me to send any communications out to any one of the divisions without his approval. Policy issues I would not send out without the Director's approval anyway, but things concerning personnel and budgetary issues, I would send out routinely. I asked him whether his directive applied to everything. He said yes.*

The interim director began a concerted effort to discredit and reduce Neil's authority and responsibility. Having once been included in all the division directors' meetings, Neil was no longer invited to them. There were weeks when he would not see his superior. He was isolated and had many of his tasks taken from him. There were closed door meetings with Neil's subordinates.

> I thought, if I am going to sit in my office and be paid my
>   salary to do some paper pushing, they must be fools.

Neil used the following strategy.

1. He talked to the director's superior who brought it to the attention of the mobber, which made things worse. Nothing was done about it. So it appeared that the mobbing was condoned by higher management. This situation lasted for over three years.

> Neil: Most people are fools. They cannot detect changes in
>   their environment. They blind themselves to change. I
>   have never done that. If you feel something is changing,
>   you need to get yourself a notebook. Put down date,
>   time, place, persons, event, and what happened.

2. Neil's response was to document every interaction with his superior. He made sure that he documented all of the director's communications and followed his requests to the letter.

> He told me that he wanted to see everything that came through
>   my office. So I sent him everything. Which was funny.
>   Because every day there were two or three dozen pieces
>   of correspondence. He couldn't handle that. They start-
>   ed piling up on his desk. So he asked my assistant,
>   "Who usually handles these materials?" She told him
>   that I did. So he came to me and told me that I had mis-
>   understood his directive. And I said, "No, I have it right
>   here in writing." I had asked him to give me this in
>   writing. I always asked him to give me his directives in
>   writing.
>
> "Well," he said, "there is a miscommunication." I
>   asked, "Is this what your intent is?" He said, "No, I
>   just want to review things of the divisions."

3. Neil then talked with an attorney about what choices were available. The attorney advised him to continue to keep a very detailed record. Initially, he felt that this would be a waste of time, because the mobber did nothing illegal. It was within his power, as a director, to reallocate tasks. However, later on, this documentation could have proved useful.

4. Neil made a conscious decision that those in the organization who were mobbing him were the ones who were "crazy", not himself. He was able to maintain enough of his self-image to withstand the attempts at intimidation. He spent less time in the office rather than more. He did not engage in futile attempts to prove his worth. Having once spent from 8 in the morning until 6 or 7 in the evening, even on the weekends at times, he now stopped doing that. He came in at 8:30 and would leave at 5. He maintained that they were foolish to pay him for not exercising his mental faculties. He devoted his time to another business to challenge his mind and experience accomplishment. He waited out the situation.

5. It is important to point out that Neil figured out what was actually going on, and did not take the mobbing personally. He used his wits and followed through with a plan of action. When one course of action appeared to be blocked, he turned to another.

Eventually, Neil's director was asked to resign. Neil could have been a casualty of the mobber's arrogance, quest for power, and attempt to oust him. There were others who did fall prey to his maneuverings. Neil did not experience long-term damage to his psyche as a result of the experience because he did not assume a victim mentality. He was a seasoned administrator possessing prior experience that guided him in withstanding the mobbing.

SURVIVAL STRATEGIES

People who have endured and survived the most extreme situations—concentration camps, torture, forced isolation—have used mental shields and never lost hope that things would change.

Some of our interview partners mentioned the following strategies that helped them to endure the situation. They:

- Figured out what actually was going on.
- Responded to the attacks with confidence and without fear.
- Did not participate in the game that was inflicted on them.
- Refused to be a victim.
- Displayed a great deal of spiritual and mental strength and trusted that things would change. They stuck it out and prepared to be there for the long haul.
- Consciously took steps to leave.
- Diverted their energies to other pursuits they enjoyed and did not invest their creativity in the organization.

We have pointed out that mobbing affects you so deeply that commonly used stress-relieving techniques, such as exercise and meditation, are not sufficient, though they may be very helpful temporarily. They may actually distract you from seeking proactive solutions such as finding a new job and empowering yourself.

We want to refer you to the many excellent self-help books that focus on building your potential, your self-confidence, that help you regain control, or deal with anger and anxiety. Examples are: *Managing Your Mind: The Mental Fitness Guide* by Gillian Butler and Tony Hope and *The Feeling Good Handbook* by David D. Burns. Judith Wyatt and Chauncey Hare give specific, step-by-step therapeutic advice on how to empower yourself to deal with workplace abuse in their book *Work Abuse: How to Recognize and Survive It*. You can find many other excellent books in the self-help section of any major bookstore.

Mobbing is a human drama that happens in many different guises. You may find novels such as *The Scarlet Letter,* or movies such as *A Few Good Men,* also helpful in giving perspective to your personal story.[2]

SOME SURVIVAL STRATEGIES

- Go through grieving consciously.
- Believe in the value of change.
- Do not isolate yourself.
- Seek out friends' and family support.
- Have a pet.
- Gain strength from things you love: flowers, music, "talismans" such as pictures, special jewelry, stones.
- Be with people and do things that build your self-esteem.
- Use your existing skills in another context, such as volunteering, or part-time job.
- Learn a new skill.
- Stop "victim" thoughts.
- Realize you are in control of yourself and you have choices.
- Distance yourself from the workplace and gain perspective.
- Make a plan.
- Have faith.

The following are some ways to deal with the effects of your experience that were used or suggested by our interview partners.

Do Not Isolate Yourself

There may be a tendency to prolong the effects of mobbing by isolating yourself. This may reinforce feelings of depression and hopelessness. We find it imperative to overcome this tendency and to ask for support, as impossible as it may seem at times. Seek help outside the work environment with members of your family, trusted friends or a carefully chosen therapist.

Engaging in recreational activities that help you maintain contact with other people, such as a bowling league, are important. Some may choose to do volunteer work. Also a pet can contribute to coping as well as healing.

Build Your Self-Esteem

Mobbing is humiliating and degrading. It affects your very core, the image of yourself. These are some important ways to strengthen or rebuild your self-esteem.

- Evaluate your many skills.
- Engage in pursuits that you enjoy.
- Pamper yourself.
- Use positive self-talk, self-affirmations.
- Maximize the time you spend with people who value you.

Internal talk is very important. Positive affirmations help you to retrieve your own internal resources, your strengths. You can focus on what strength you have and develop an attitude of gratitude.

Joan: *You wonder, 'Why bother? What is the point?' You go through those kinds of feelings, up and down. I had to get my perspective back. I had to tell myself, 'My kids are OK. It is warm in here. There is food in the refrigerator. There still is money in the bank. The dog is wagging his tail.'*

Deal with Anger, Loss and Betrayal

Howard: *I am told by my spirituality that you cannot be vin-dictive. That you destroy yourself if you hate. I have to rationalize it. They could give me a million dollars. It would not be worth what I have had to go through these last three years.*

Anger is prompted by hurt, betrayal, and fear. Anger turned inward can be self-destructive and corroborate the effects of the stress caused by the mobbing experience. Misdirected at innocent others, it can destroy one's relationships. The energy that anger generates, focused in a positive direction, can pull you along until you are at an even and more stable place within yourself. Then the anger must be released. Our interview partners shared some of the strategies they used.

Writing

Joan: *I used my anger to enable myself to get through this faster, by looking forward and not backward. It was not easy. But sitting and feeling sorry for yourself is not what I consider to be time well spent.*

Write about your feelings, your situation, yourself. Use whatever language you wish however out of character it may be. It's okay. You can save or destroy your writing.

Create Quiet Times

Occasionally, set aside a time when you can be alone. Use dim light or candles, perhaps with soft music. Allow yourself to fully and completely feel all the hurt and sadness and aloneness. Feel the gentle healing that comes with grief.

Private Screaming

Joan: *There is a technique that I have used since I was a child.
I will go off by myself somewhere in the countryside,
somewhere where there is no one around. I will scream.
I will cry. I release all of it. It feels like you are losing
your mind, but actually you are regaining it. It's sort of
a self-induced primal scream therapy. After I'm fin-
ished, I'm fine.*

Movement

Regular exercise and any type of movement is important. Controlled,
strenuous exercise releases endorphins that make you feel better.
When you feel so low that you can't make yourself work out, find
people who will go with you. Howard expressed how difficult movement becomes in such circumstances:

*I eat more. I have never been so lethargic and so
demotivated. I do believe in exercise, but I haven't
exercised much.*

Do something that needs to be done but does not take a lot of
emotion, physical strength, or a lot of thinking. Just going through
the motions helps. Getting things started, the first steps, can take you
to the next level—the feeling of accomplishment. Getting up, moving around, cleaning the shower, doing the dishes, the laundry. Clean
out a closet, clean out the car, the basement, anything you have
wanted to do for a long time. One thing can make all the difference.
And cleaning and organizing can take on a symbolic meaning:
You gain control and you straighten things out. And you
accomplish something.

THINGS YOU LOVE

Surround yourself with things you love; flowers, music, special
objects. Some of our interview partners used keepsakes or talismans.
We refer to talismans as anything that exerts a powerful, positive

influence on your thoughts, feelings, and actions. Talismans give you a special force through the faith and love others have for you.

Some people wore or kept a ring, pin or a small item, even a card, from a significant relative, friend, in their pocket, or on their night-stand. These symbols signify some other place in life where the person is accepted, appreciated unconditionally.

KEEP A SENSE OF PERSPECTIVE

Tragedies are part of life: illness, deaths, losing a job, natural disasters, accidents, betrayal, divorce. You may never be prepared to deal with them. We suggest that everyone should prepare to deal with tragedies. For some, their faith might be a sufficient grounding. Others may prepare like the Red Cross prepares for disaster—with shelters, with helpers, with food reserves, blankets and clean water supplies. Trust that you can deal with any situation that happens to you, whatever might come your way. Anticipate what your options might be, how you may react, and where you can get help.

Jack: *There were some changes coming, and I thought I could ride it out, deal with it. Four years ago we bought this other business to develop so that eventually I could afford to get out.*

GE: *So you planned an escape, four years before you left, when you knew this was going to happen?*

Jack: *I intended to remain as stable as I could there until this place got to the point that it could support us. I knew that it was an inevitable situation. I think that helped in the emotional part.*

GE: *You were building something else to go to. You had a plan.*

Jack: *Right.*

Once individuals understand the mobbing process, they can prepare to deal with it and work on a plan. The plan might simply be, "I trust my experience and my capabilities, no matter what. I know I can do it. I can find another job, if I want to. I know I need time. I know I need to act in a manner that values my health."

> Jack: *I feel really fortunate that we had spent the three or four years getting ready for it because it was a natural move then.*
>
> GE: *If you hadn't done that. . ?*
>
> Jack: *Oh, God...oh, man...*

Understanding that this is a recognized workplace syndrome that has a name, and that the individuals are not responsible for the evil being directed towards them, has helped our interview partners gain a different perspective of their experience.

Keep in mind that there may be gender differences in how persons can best cope. It may be more difficult for some men to try some of our suggestions, such as screaming or gaining strength from talismans. And it may not be easy for women to distance themselves from the workplace.

The most important element is to believe in change and never lose faith in your abilities and life experience. This will carry you through and enable you to gain strength.

THE POWER OF HUMOR

Although there is nothing at all funny about what is happening to you as a result of the mobbing process, humor can be an effective way of reducing anxiety, maintaining balance, and gaining distance. Humorous experiences are pleasant or joyful and are considered to contribute to feelings of well being and mental health.

One of our interview partners was given a thick sheaf of papers all containing a variety of jokes pulled off the Internet by a family member. "I got lost in the jokes," she said, "and even if some of them weren't all that funny, I found myself laughing hard."

Laughter dilates the cardio-vascular system, increasing the flow of blood and oxygen to all parts of the body. It exercises the respiratory system; the abdominal muscles contract and relax, massaging vital organs—"internal jogging", as Norman Cousins said. The brain releases the body's natural pain-killing substances, the endorphins, and provides access to "that apothecary inside you."[3] This may be why we feel better after a good laugh.

We recommend looking for humor, not necessarily in your situation, but in other simple day to day life situations—opportunities to laugh. This also helps focus attention away from yourself and onto something else for awhile.

CHOOSE PROFESSIONAL HELP VERY CAUTIOUSLY

Professional help is essential. Yet, not all therapists are knowledgeable enough about the devastating effects of work abuse. Leymann suggests that an extended mobbing process may cause a destruction of the personality. He points out that it is not possible to evaluate a victim's original personality as long as this individual is suffering from post-traumatic stress disorder (PTSD).

Consequently, professionals not trained to diagnose PTSD, or not familiar with workplace abuse and mobbing as a possible cause for PTSD, may make false assumptions. They may hold the patients responsible for their situation, labeling them as having a certain susceptibility or preexisting personality problem.

Thus, therapists might actually reinforce the patients' distress. Judith Wyatt and Chauncey Hare developed particular therapeutic procedures and instructions—aimed at re-establishing personal power and described in detail in their 1997 book, *Work Abuse*. They tell how to choose a therapist, explain a possible therapeutic process, give step-by-step instructions on how to deal with workplace abuse, and advise therapists how they can best help their patients.

CONSIDERATIONS FOR LEGAL RECOURSE

If you are suffering through the pain and fears of a mobbing situation at your workplace, you may wonder what legal rights you have.

Because mobbing in the workplace and its grave impact on the victim have not been recognized, mobbees feel that they are somehow at fault and therefore have little recourse. Most of our interview partners agonized over whether they should seek legal redress.

Concerns That May Keep You From Taking Legal Action

As a mobbing victim, you may think of many reasons not to seek legal redress.

- Since you have no written contract, you believe you have no recourse.

- You have not documented every instance of mobbing behavior.

- In a vulnerable state, you may find the task of finding a competent, trusted attorney overwhelming.

- Legal recourse is expensive, stressful, and can take several years to complete. Companies often have attorneys on staff and the ability to fight a case for years.

- What about your reputation? You may not find another job in your field, if other employers learn you have filed a lawsuit. You do not wish to undergo the public scrutiny and add further embarrassment to the humiliation of losing your job, especially when you think you may have been at fault.

- Loyalty to your organization and your work and the desire to do no harm to the employer, in spite of the mobbing, is causing you conflict.

- Family members and friends convey the belief that you will be worse off in the end, and will most likely walk away with less than when you started. Their advice—"Get out!" "Resign!" "Move on!"

- There is a real personal and financial cost to seeking a legal remedy and the outcome is, by its very nature, uncertain and stress-promoting.

Considerations That May Lead You to Decide to Take Legal Action

- ◆ You do not want to be victimized.

- ◆ You want to stand up for your rights and those of others.

- ◆ You have diligently documented the mobbing behaviors.

- ◆ You want/need a financial package that compensates you in your transition.

- ◆ You want your employer to be more vigilant in preventing future occurrences.

If you weigh all of these considerations carefully, and come to the conclusion that you want to go ahead in pursuing legal redress, then we suggest the following.

Simply Put—Begin

If you are being mobbed, you should document date, time, place, who was involved, and what happened. Keep a diary. Begin outlining your mobbing issues on paper as clearly as possible. If you are unable to write down your thoughts because you are so distraught, have an understanding and trusted friend help, if possible. Then visit an attorney as well prepared as you can. Good attorneys will be able to support you empathically and will understand what you are trying to say.

You should ask what his/her fee and other costs will be and what kind of payment arrangements can be made. Even if you must borrow from family and friends, it may well be worth it, if you believe you have cause for legal action.

It is always wise to keep your visit confidential, especially from everyone in your office. If your employer learns you are consulting an attorney, action may be taken to quickly terminate you.

A Word of Caution

When an attorney agrees to take your case, it is usually with the belief that you have a case that can be won. But no matter how competent your attorney is, nor how good your case appears to be, there are no guarantees that you will win in our legal system.

Mediated Settlement: A Good Option?

If you are able to mediate a reasonable settlement early on, you may be wise to do so. Otherwise, you risk a prolonged court process which brings further mental and financial stress and may even end in loss of your case. Your settlement may include a severance payment, outstanding vacation time, benefits such as health, life and disability insurance, and pension for whatever period seems appropriate in your case. You may also want to negotiate a letter of recommendation, references, and other matters that may be applicable in your case, such as an agreement not to contest unemployment benefits.

REMEMBER THE POSSIBILITIES

We are fortunate to live in a society where there are countless possibilities. Success is always possible. But each person has to determine his or her own standard of what success means. Success for one might mean being a decent person, helping other people, and living by one's values. Success for another might be to have a loving marriage, or great kids, or to be on good terms with one's god.

Understand that you have educated yourself throughout your life. It is not the job that makes you who you are, you make the job. In fact, we suggest that many persons who started their own businesses may have been victims of mobbing. Because they could not trust to work within another company and they had the strength to transcend their experience, they developed their unique gifts and ventured out on their own.

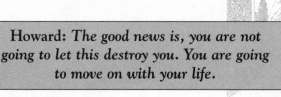

Howard: *The good news is, you are not going to let this destroy you. You are going to move on with your life.*

RECOVERING AND MOVING FORWARD

Howard: *What are we doing with our lives to move on? How do we deal with the basic premise that we are responsible for our own behavior? I have three kids who are college graduates. They say, "Put it behind you."*

Withstanding mobbing, and healing after its occurrence, depend on many factors:

- How gravely were you injured?
- How quickly were you able to realize what was happening to you?
- Are your friends and family able to help?
- How much has your personality and health been altered by the experience?
- How effective is your therapy?
- Are you or have you been able to find and engage in another employment or activity in a nurturing environment, where you are appreciated and successful?

Howard, following months of emotional paralysis, found a temporary position in which he was well respected. Jack developed his own business, as several others did. Ron, however, never re-entered the workforce, although he was hired as a consultant in another country for several months.

Judy, after two years of severe depression, found an executive position in another city that built on her past professional experience. She said:

I can't believe how nice everyone is. And they act like I know something. I am getting my confidence back.

Chapter 4 Endnotes

1. Golden, Tom. *Swallowed by A Snake: The Gift of the Masculine Side of Healing*, 1996.

2. See the list of some 25 movies with the mobbing theme in *Eliminating Professors* by Dr. K. Westhues, 1999.

3. Cousins, 1979.

FIVE

Family and Friends
How They Are Affected
How They Can Help

> Be my angel of light.
> Come, take my hand.
> If I am unable to reach out,
> still, I need the touch,
> warm clasp, a friend.
>
> —Gail Pursell Elliott

> You can never completely humiliate a person who is
> loved at home.
>
> —Kenneth Westhues
> *Eliminating Professors*

In this chapter, we shift focus. We want to explain to family and friends—the most important support system for the victims—what is happening with their loved ones who are experiencing mobbing. We list early warning signs and suggest ways that victims can best be assisted to find their way out of the maze of despair.

To the victims we want to say, "Your family and friends are not used to you being so different and they do not know how to deal with you. They do not really know or understand what is going on, even if you tell them. They may feel helpless, too."

WHAT IS HAPPENING?

When someone is very ill, others can usually empathize and know how to help. They may call, send a card of encouragement, or flowers. But in a mobbing, they often do not do anything.

The turmoil and confusion that mobbed persons experience for so long affect not only their own sense of self and changes their behavior, it also affects all their important relationships. While some mobbees withdraw, others feel a need to talk about their experiences incessantly. They seek approval of their thoughts, points of view, and grasp for much needed sympathy. They reiterate their story hoping to receive support. Partners, family, and friends can feel overwhelmed by hearing the same story over and over again. Soon they may begin to withdraw.

They wonder: "What is the matter?" "Why is he so irritable?" "Why doesn't she call us anymore?" "Why is she depressed?"

Diana: *I remember when I was so distraught, I looked at my daughters and saw that they were worried. I still remember their faces. Their inability to make me better made them sad.*

Howard: *My children can't quite figure out what happened to their father. My kids are saying to me, "You are supposed to take every one of these things as a challenge, Dad, as an opportunity to be better."*

Joan: *I had my crying spells. I isolated myself. I didn't want my children to see me cry. I don't know if they knew it or not.*

Judy: *I started going to church. There is no one to talk to. Who do you tell about this that wants to hear? Nobody. And of course you do not let anybody know what is going on because you feel humiliated, isolated.*

Catherine: *You hide your feelings, pretend that everything is
OK. You play a game, so they act on the basis of the
game that you play.*

Judy: *And so you make the situation worse.*

NOT THE USUAL SELF

Victims are far from being their usual selves. Feeling shame, anguish
and even guilt, some withdraw into a depression and isolate
themselves. Some mobbees cannot reveal their agony and rarely
do they understand the complex situation themselves. They are in
disbelief and feel confused.

Howard: *So I am asking myself, why am I so dysfunctional?
I got through life this far, and then all of a sudden I
am not functional. I do not want to admit that I am
dysfunctional.*

EARLY WARNING SIGNS—
CHANGES IN BEHAVIORS

The following are behaviors that
may seem unusual for your loved
one. Recognize that, all things
being equal, your loved one or
friend may be experiencing a major
crisis at work. If uncharacteristic
behaviors persist, they may signal a
mobbing experience. Do not ignore
them. Take them seriously.

> **You do not let anybody know
> what is going on because you feel
> humiliated, isolated.**

121

CHANGED BEHAVIORS

- Reiterating office stories or obsessing about peoples' behaviors at the workplace.
- Becoming silent or talking less.
- Excessive negativism.
- Fearfulness, suspicion, anxiety.
- Crying spells.
- Irritability.
- Expressions of uncontrolled rage.
- Hiding, isolation.
- Attempting to hide feelings.
- Refusing help.
- Requesting support, becoming needy.
- Loss of concentration, unable to read for any length of time.
- Forgetfulness.
- Fatigue.
- Constant physical movement.
- Moving and speaking slower.
- Exercise, too much or no more exercise.
- Changed eating habits, too much or very little.
- Increased smoking.
- Having sleeping difficulties.
- Developing compulsive obsessive behaviors, like excessive shopping, excessive cleaning.
- Excessive mess in their rooms, kitchens, homes.
- Failure to pay bills.
- Change in outer appearance, such as dress, hygiene, etc.
- Change in expression, looking haunted.
- Proneness to accidents, injuries.
- Developing potentially severe medical problems.

THE DIFFICULTY OF COMMUNICATING
AND GIVING SUPPORT

As we mentioned earlier, mobbees feel that they have lost their professional dignity and that they have experienced a death of their own selves. The mobbing shattered the image of who they used to be.

They often go through grieving and they experience intense emotions as they come to grips with their loss and their uncertain future. They will show grieving reactions: anger, fear, denial, bargaining, and acceptance. Grief is a process that takes time. Some people fall into silence and may need to isolate themselves for a while. Others engage in any type of action or busy work as a way to get control over some things. They may begin to work on their legal defense. Some people do not communicate openly, isolate themselves, build up defenses, and thus place tremendous strain on the family.

Others, not knowing whom to trust, may develop a suspicious attitude. This, above all, compounds the confusion among their loved ones and creates entangled communication patterns. In such circumstances, conflicts at home may abound and escalate.

Supportive communication—listening to each other's thoughts and feelings—is a way to help disentangle, to share thoughts and emotions. But often this does not seem possible, as simple as it may be.

> Joan: *I tried to talk to my mother, but she said, "You need to tell all this to your counselor." And I said, "You know, if I had someone in my family I could talk to, I would not need a counselor. But you do not want to hear it, you do not want to listen." She could not. Because she became terribly upset. It has impacted her more than I even know. It has a ripple effect on relationships.*

As a crisis lingers on, partners may feel overwhelmed by continuously being cast into the care-giver role and being unable to eliminate the actual problem. They too become needy and can't receive support. It is this imbalance, over too long a period, that may eventually lead to separation or divorce.

John's wife: *I emotionally supported him for many years, and then I couldn't do it any longer. I started to ignore him. I wanted to run away. When he was at home, he just sat on the sofa, writing down these incidents. Then he would put on earphones and listen to music—to stop obsessing, I suppose. It made me crazy. He became invisible to me because I could not stand to see him like this. Every day he went into a crazy workplace. And every day I wanted to run away.*

Joan: *I was still married. My husband, instead of giving me what I needed, to just put his arms around me and tell me, "Everything will be all right," and hold me for a while, told me: "Maybe you need to see a counselor." I did not get the nurturing that I needed. I came home one evening from a really rough day. Immediately, my husband said he was going to the movies and that he would catch up with me later.*

Allan's wife: *I got really tired of hearing the same story over and over and over again. This went on year after year. Finally it dawned on me that I couldn't do this any longer. He needed to try to find solutions with someone else.*

It is a lot to ask of family and friends to give support over long periods of time. They may feel overwhelmed as well. Seeing a loved one in pain and in crisis, fearful and continuously anxious, they may feel powerless and may not know how to help. Both must work to understand what the other needs. This will support relationships during and after the mobbing.

Luis' wife: *I had a terrible time getting over my outrage. I'm just beginning to cope with that. I felt it was so unjust. In my heart of hearts I don't want to be vindictive, but you want to see justice done. It breaks your heart to see*

a member of your own family treated so unjustly. I find
myself angry and irritable and feeling helpless, because
there is nothing that I can do to change this. It seems so
unreal. It's like you're looking at a horror picture on the
late show.

Occasionally, efforts by family and friends may seem futile. Some individuals cannot find the strength to accept the support that is cast like a safety net around them. We have seen several persons with loving support systems, yet they feel continuously bad about themselves, paralyzed or suicidal. Suggesting professional counseling can be helpful, even necessary. An offer to call a therapist or take them there may be what they need. However, be aware that this, especially coming from a significant other, may reinforce the feeling of a lack of self-worth. If the victim refuses, family members might consider going themselves to be better able to deal with some of the out-of-character behavior of the mobbed victim. Giving time, having patience and faith are important ingredients to make it through this experience.

If at all feasible, the most essential form of support could be that which would enable the victim to leave the "battlefield."

Catherine: *It was really important that my husband immedi-*
ately understood and encouraged me to get out, to resign
and develop my own business. I would not have done
this without his encouragement.

Allan: *I could not have done this without my wife. She was*
very helpful and supportive, and she had some good
ideas. I was very fortunate that she was in my life—and
she still is.

Luis: *I think I've gotten all the support I can handle. I don't*
think there's anything my family could do differently.

AFFIRMATION IS KEY

Joan: *I felt ashamed, I felt embarrassed, I felt confused. I felt afraid to go downtown to go shopping because I might run into somebody.*

The most important support family and friends can give lies in affirming the person, their strengths, their character, their courage, their achievements. They must demonstrate their love in every way they know how. This will help the person to rebuild his or her identity.

Joan: *I went home to visit my family on the West Coast, and it was therapeutic. They didn't bring up the subject of a job. I was greeted with love and acceptance. They pampered me and made me laugh.*

THE HELPING ART OF BEING THERE

Just knowing that there is a person who cares, understands and accepts the individual the way he or she is, makes all the difference.

S. C. Mahoney in *The Art of Helping People Effectively* explains a concept called "the helping art of presence." Simply put, this is just "being there" in an accepting and receptive frame of mind, well attuned to the person's needs at the moment, doing and saying very little. Its effectiveness lies in what we convey through our presence alone.

You can take someone out to eat, to a bookstore, go for a walk—just lending them your spirit. Ultimately, this will help them grow in strength.

Our interview partners expressed what they found helpful:

Joan: *One friend said to me, "For the next 90 days you may say anything you want. You may repeat yourself over*

*and over and over again, and I will listen to you even if
you repeat some of the same stories 18 times. And if
you do not want me to do anything but say "hum" I will
do that. I will not mind. Just get it out. But then after
the end of 90 days, let's make a plan to move forward."*

Diana: *What was so significant for me was having somebody
call me up and say, "Hey, what are you doing?" Well
knowing that I was not doing anything, they would say,
"Lets go out to eat, I'm buying." It was the idea that
someone was caring. We would go out and laugh and
eat something that tasted good. I think if that could
happen often during this experience, it would really help.*

Joan: *One of the hardest things was to ask for help. I do not
ask for stuff. This is the way I was raised. I ask very
little of people, so I did not get very much. Many people
are waiting for someone to ask.*

Judy: *There was one person at church who called me often,
sent me cards. That meant something.*

Luis: *Just absolute support—knowing that they are there.*

Friends and family may need to attempt to influence their loved
one to seek and prepare for alternatives with questions such as: "How
long do you think you can survive in this situation? What would your
life look like if you decided to leave this job today? How would you
be different? What would change?"

Diana: *I had a friend in California who called me and said,
"Remember, Diana, there is a big world out there."*

LENDING SUPPORT
SOME THINGS FAMILY AND FRIENDS CAN DO

- LISTEN.
- Help identify the mobbing phenomenon.
- Suggest therapy and provide names of therapists. Offer to call.
- Recommend a visit to the doctor. Suggest that medication may be helpful.
- Suggest to seek legal advice. Offer lawyers' names and offer to make an appointment.
- Suggest ways to keep finances under control.
- Advise to look for other job opportunities early, to plan the escape.
- Help work on a resume and suggest work opportunities.
- Invite your friend to join you in networking.
- Suggest joint activities like going to the movies, to dinner, or going for a walk.
- Call, send a card or flowers.
- Recommend or bring helpful books.
- Practice the helping art of presence.
- LISTEN.

Remember the possibilities.

Supportive Listening— Using Helpful Language

When you engage in supportive listening, it is important to be aware that not all language, as well as it is meant, is helpful. There are some phrases that are more affirmative than others and help individuals find their own solutions.

NOT HELPFUL LANGUAGE	HELPFUL LANGUAGE
That just wasn't the job for you.	How are you doing with all this?
You must have done something to cause this.	How can I help?
You'll feel worse before you feel better.	Please tell me what you are feeling.
You have your whole life ahead of you.	This must be hard for you.
I don't want to hear about it again.	What's the hardest part for you?
Call me when I can help.	I'll call you tomorrow.
Just get over it!	You must really be hurting.
You've already told me that twice.	You must really feel angry.
It's time to put it behind you.	Take all the time you need.
Think of your responsibilities.	What do you want most of all?
Be strong!	Thank you for sharing your feelings.
	Remember the possibilities.

SIX

Organizations
How They Are Affected
What They Can Do

It is not a coincidence that companies that win service and quality awards are the same ones that emphasize the ethics of employee treatment.

—Emily S. Bassman
Abuse in the Workplace;
Management Remedies and Bottom Line Impact

Although what you call "mobbing behaviors" do exist, we do not condone them. We have clear Principles of Behavior and employees understand that behaviors that violate those Principles will be addressed.

—Robin Winburn
Human Resources Policy Planner, Levi Strauss & Co.

———————————————— ♦ ————————————————

When the mobbing syndrome strikes an organization, the costs measured in productivity, morale, human suffering, and dollars can be high. Teamwork becomes difficult as people turn their focus from the goals and tasks of the organization to internal maneuvering and survival tactics.

In the following section, we address a number of warning signals that may help organizations recognize mobbing.

It is important to distinguish between organizations that use mobbing as a strategy, i.e., top management participates in the mobbing, and those in which mobbing happens without the intent or knowledge of the leadership. It may be that leaders are unaware, have been kept in the dark, or have not been informed correctly of the spiraling events that may have led to the expulsion of an employee. Mobbing can only exist if management condones it.

ALL TYPES OF ORGANIZATIONS

Mobbing can occur in all types of organizations and industries. It can occur in large or small companies, in government, in nonprofits, in the healthcare industry, in education. Anywhere. As noted earlier, smaller organizations and nonprofits may be more susceptible to mobbing because there may be fewer protective mechanisms in place. It also appears that mobbing may be quite prevalent in health-care and in higher education, as the title of Kenneth Westhues' 1998 book *Eliminating Professors* indicates.

However, the more organizations are striving to achieve excellence through teamwork, empowerment, trust, honesty, open and frequent communication, staff development, and established grievance and conflict resolution practices, the higher the probability that mobbing can be prevented.

WARNING SIGNALS

Significant Changes Without Preparing Employees

Change causes fear and uncertainty. Change that happens without adequate information and preparation, and without the cooperation and participation of employees, may be a cause for mobbing.

One Individual Has Suddenly Become a Target

Most organizations have a "rumor mill." However, when rumors begin to include attacks on a person's personal or professional reputation, made either humorously or as whispered criticism, this can be an indication that a mobbing is in progress.

Howard sided with a colleague whom he perceived as being mobbed. *I was asked by my boss: "Why are you talking to her? You show compassion for her," is the message I got. He ridiculed her. They would laugh, roll their eyes. Dehumanizing. Demoralizing. I was a basket case. She was a basket case.*

Sean's co-worker: *These people did not help us that day. They made demands. The way they stated things was not in a nice way. They were on him like glue. It looked like a set up. It looked like they were trying to provoke him. It made me angry to have to sit there and keep my mouth shut. I was afraid that I was going to be fired if I said something to them about it. The manager told me the next day to "Grin and bear it," and a co-worker added, "If you want to keep your job."*

These people came back after he was fired. They were a lot nicer and made suggestions instead of commands and demands. This made me even angrier. It confirmed my belief that they had come that day to set him up to be fired.

Earlier, we mentioned the situation of a new boss or supervisor who may begin to mob individuals whom he perceives as threatening. The mobber questions their decisions, judges and discredits work that up to this point had been quite satisfactory, if not superior.

Judy: *I had been with the company since 1983 through 1994. Most of the people targeted were my age and had a long tenure. We had performed well, generally. The kind of things that you quantify, we had performed well. One day we got these evaluations. They were all horrible. They came from nowhere. I cried.*

A new boss may convey the impression that he or she is the authority now setting a new standard for the company.

Howard: *I had been with the company for years. From the day the new CEO came in the door, from that day, he treated me like dirt.*

Judy: *I had a new boss and his approach was very demeaning. My meetings with him included my secretary. This is sort of non-traditional. With my secretary present he would say things like, "Everybody is complaining that you do not return calls." And I said, "Everybody? Who?"*

Because if there is anything I did, it was to return calls. I was on the phone eight hours a day. So for him to say to me, "You are not returning calls," was like, "What?" For me, who returns calls on the weekend, in the evenings. I said, "Who?" He said: "Everybody." I said, "I cannot respond to this. I do not know what you are talking about." Then he said, "You better take good note because I am going to be watching you."

Alliances Across the Hierarchy

The syndrome may appear as individuals on upper levels of management begin jockeying for position or playing internal political games. The behavior may then involve subordinates as the mobber begins to undermine the victim.

Joan: *When you're being blind-sided, you know when people are trying to undermine you. How to stop it, how to confront it are entirely different things. This individual was in a position in which he was able to become friendly with my direct subordinates. And the closer he got to them, the farther they got from me.*

Subordinates may align themselves with the mobber on a higher management level for a variety of reasons, and especially to protect their jobs.

> Joan: *I knew when I established standards and they were not followed by my direct subordinates, someone told them: "It's all right," or "Don't do it," or "You don't have to listen to her. She's not going to be around much longer. You come to me, if there's something that you don't like."*

> Judy: *It was obvious what was going on. I heard the CEO tell the secretaries not to do any work for him. Then he could not get his work done by the deadline.*

> Luis: *They don't understand what they have destroyed. They think they're doing the right thing based upon a false fear—based upon lies that they have been told.*

"Anarchy"

Anarchy may be a by-product or deliberately instigated as a mobbing tactic. Mobbers may think that once the victim is gone the employees will extend him or her their allegiance. The focus of those involved is no longer the work at hand or the goals of the organization. The focus has shifted to a personal alliance.

> Joan: *This person thought he could come in and put in his own system after destroying everything I had built. He thought that people would then support him. He created anarchy in order to oust me. He was not able to establish order. He was not able to establish standards. He was not able to establish anything.*

As organizations lose key individuals, experience a sudden increase in turnover, internal dissension, and/or low morale as a result of mobbing, they may attempt to correct the situation, without

135

dealing with core issues. This can further complicate and weaken the very structures that they are attempting to strengthen.

Use of Consultants

The internal problems may prompt the management to bring in a consultant to assess the situation. This not only creates further dollar costs, but may be used as an excuse for management to continue the mobbing.

Ironically, for the assessment to be "fair and impartial," the victim may be isolated further by being removed from the workplace, forbidden to communicate with any co-workers, or to be on company grounds during the assessment. A fair investigation would contact all the people involved, and hear all people out, but this was not what happened in Joan's case.

> Joan: *I was not allowed to see a list of the concerns and complaints against me. I was not allowed to speak to anybody, any current or former staff, under threat of immediate termination.*
>
> *Many staff had no idea of what was going on, where I was, what had happened to me. They brought in an outside human resource person to do an "impartial" assessment. Others were allowed to talk among them-selves prior to her arrival, but I was allowed to address no one.*
>
> *I was hung before I had a chance to speak or even know what the concerns were.*
>
> *Two of the perpetrators—they were at the corporate level—got to the consultant and talked to her privately. I could not speak openly with her because one of these two sat in on our conversation, stared at me and took notes the whole time. The letter that went out was pre-sented in a negative fashion so that the only people who showed up were people who had complaints, except for one. He was later terminated by the same people who had mobbed me.*

The need for the assessment may be based upon rumor, innuendo, or hearsay. Individuals may not be made aware of the allegations against them until after the process has been completed. At that point, a determination has been made that is usually unalterable by any information they present to defend their position. Individuals are presumed guilty by virtue of the evidence orchestrated and presented by others, are offered no support or representation, and frequently are refused the right to face their accusers. The person must comply or be terminated from employment. They are denied due process.

WARNING SIGNALS CHECKLIST

1. Are the problems of a department being blamed on one individual?

2. Is the person now accused of substandard performance or some other unacceptable behavior someone whose work and behavior was previously above average?

3. Are people, particularly in higher management, not fully qualified or experienced to hold the positions they hold?

4. Are there sudden losses of key individuals?

5. Is there an unusually high staff turnover?

6. Is there increased sick leave?

7. Is the company experiencing unexplainable low morale?

8. Has the company suddenly experienced change of any kind, such as restructuring, new staff and leadership, or new procedures? Has there been insufficient time to inform, involve, and train employees adequately?

A HOUSE OF CARDS

Luis: *While I was out of town, an unscheduled board meeting took place instigated by the key staff who were trying to discredit me. They got me on the phone and confronted me with a flood of accusations that I was able later to refute with documented examples. Our board chairman had a mild heart attack over it and later resigned.*

It affected a lot of employees who now are leaving. Key people, some of the best people we ever had, are now gone. And they were not subjected to anything other than witnessing what was going on.

The following paragraphs describe the effects of mobbing on the organization itself. Like a house of cards collapsing with the slightest disturbance, organizations experience similar disintegration when mobbing is prevalent. They have a hard time recovering, even after mobbing has been halted. And the repercussions affect the bottom line.

Luis: *I'm actually more worried about the company at this point than about what might happen to me. I think that the progress of at least the last four years has been destroyed.*

REPERCUSSIONS

- Reduction in quality and quantity of work.
- Unpleasant employee relations, including breakdown of communications and teamwork.
- Factionalism.
- Increased employee turnover.
- Increased sick leave.
- Loss of reputation, credibility.
- Cost of consultants.
- Unemployment insurance claims, workers' compensation/disability, occupational stress claims.
- Settlement, litigation.

Reduction in Quality and Quantity of Work

Not only are the victims affected. It also damages teamwork and the cohesiveness necessary to accomplish good work. Furthermore, losing key staff suddenly affects the core of an organization.

> Diana: *After I left, the number of projects that were completed successfully were decreased by more than half. Affiliated organizations also started to complain about the poor service that was now provided.*

> Joan: *The systems and structure were destroyed so there would be no record.*

> Neil: *There was an important office for policy development. He just let that languish. He took funds away from them, and gradually four people left. He closed the operation down, not because it was not functional and very effective, but because it was something the former director had devised.*

Loss of Organization's Reputation

> Catherine: *The disintegration of the company was pretty significant. Several top people left. So significant, in fact, that the CEO was asked for his resignation one year after his appointment. The damage caused by his actions continue to impact the company, which has had to downsize due to significant losses in revenue, and no longer holds the leadership position in the industry that it once had.*

Increased Employee Turnover

Sensitive employees who cannot stand to watch the mobbing doubt that things will improve. They look for a better workplace and feel that they cannot really trust anyone. Costs accrue due to increased turnover, new training, loss of acquired experience.

Increased Sick Leave

Relief from the mobbing scene is often sought by legitimate sick leave. Frequent and longer leaves are costly and disruptive, and reduce productivity. In addition to the victim, others in the organization also require sick leave to escape the poisonous atmosphere.

> Diana: *An environment of fear and danger was created. Nobody ever knew who the next victim would be. Some employees tried to become invisible. But the repercussions on many staff members' health were evident. One colleague lost her hair and had to wear a wig. Another had several accidents. Others experienced new health problems.*

Unemployment Insurance Claims

Victims of mobbing may be able to claim unemployment insurance benefits. They must demonstrate that there was a forced resignation or questionable termination. Such claims constitute an additional burden on the employer.

Workers' Compensation

Some individuals are emotionally and physically so ill that they have to go on disability and are unable to ever return to the workforce.

Several states also recognize workers' compensation claims when job-related mental stress produces a physical or mental ailment. This is generally called mental-mental injury, i.e., mental stress that causes mental injury.

Studies published by the California Worker's Compensation Institute in 1994 showed a significant rise in the number of stress-related worker's compensation claims being filed. In all probability, California reflects an emerging national trend. At this time, we do not know how many of these may be due to mobbing.[1]

Litigation or Settlement

Litigation or settlement adds further costs. A victim may have ample grounds to sue a company based on discrimination, harassment, or hostile environment charges, and possibly, based on mental-mental injury. Furthermore, additional legal ground may exist when an individual's reputation has been slandered. This is presented in more detail in Chapter 8.

Luis: *The slander is a tricky thing. It's so damaging, but when it's based on rumor, it's hard to pin down who to sue. And the rumors continue to escalate even now. It's just ludicrous. My lawyer said: "You want your name cleared. You want your money." But when you're dealing with slander, that can go on for years and years.*

PREVENTION

What can an organization do to prevent mobbing from happening? The following twelve components of organizational management contribute to creating a caring and nourishing environment that can prevent the mobbing syndrome:

REDUCING THE RISK OF MOBBING
Twelve Components for Creating a Caring and Nourishing Environment

1. Mission statement that includes the organizational objectives and how employees are treated. Vision and values statements that align all employees.

2. Organizational structure: Clear reporting levels.

3. Job descriptions: Defined in terms of duties and responsibilities.

4. Personnel policies: Comprehensive, consistent, legal, simple, including expected behaviors and standards of ethics.

5. Disciplinary issues: Dealt with consistently, fairly, and expeditiously.

6. Employees buy into the goals and objectives of the organization. They have been educated regarding their role in the achievement of those goals.

7. New employees are not only selected based on their technical qualifications but also on the basis of their emotional intelligence, such as their capability of dealing with diversity, working in self-directed teams, and managing conflict.

8. Training and staff development: Highly valued for all employees. The system meets the needs of the changing organization. Training includes issues of human relations in addition to technical knowledge.

9. Communications: Open, honest, effective, and timely.

10. Participation, teamwork, creativity, decision making, trust, empowerment: Structures that allow for the highest possible degree of employees' personal involvement in achieving the company's goals.

11. Conflict resolution/mediation: A mechanism is in place for resolving conflict at all levels. There is follow-up to insure that the conflict has really been resolved.

12. Employee Assistance Programs: The company has an EAP Program. In absence of that, a comparable program may be offered, including behavioral risk assessment and management.

Awareness on the part of significant players in the organization, along with a procedure to quickly intercept the activity and start procedures for resolution, are necessary.

Giving It a Name—Creating Awareness

Sexual harassment laws existed before Anita Hill. However, because of the prominence of her story, a new awareness of sexual harassment at the workplace was created. Since then, sexual harassment policies and behavioral rules have been established in practically every workplace.

Likewise, emotional abuse is not a new phenomenon in the workplace. However, by providing a name—mobbing—and creating awareness of its ramifications, the organization can take steps towards its prevention.

Education and Training

Employees need to be sensitized and trained to identify the first signs of a mobbing process. Company policy should give clear guidance for actions to take without fearing retaliation.

Practical experiences in Sweden are numerous. The National Board of Occupational Safety and Health (NBOSH) in Stockholm has published and distributed Leymann's educational material since 1989, containing a video, overheads, manual, books, etc. Hundreds of companies have used it, according to information from NBOSH. [2]

Establishing an Anti-Mobbing Policy

Establishing an anti-mobbing policy can be compared to the development of any organizational policy that establishes the norms of acceptable conduct, such as on sexual harassment, drug or alcohol abuse, etc. The following is an example of an anti-mobbing policy that companies may wish to consider.

Example
ANTI-MOBBING POLICY

As an employee of this Organization, you are expected to adhere to acceptable conduct at all times. This involves respecting the rights and feelings of others and refraining from any behavior that might be harmful to your co-workers.

The Organization strongly supports the rights of all employees to work in an environment free from mobbing.

Mobbing is verbal or physical conduct that over a period of time, continuously and systematically:

1. **intimidates, shows hostility, threatens, and offends any co-worker;**
2. **interferes with a co-worker's performance;**
3. **otherwise adversely affects a co-worker.**

Mobbing conduct includes, but is not limited to:

- threatening, intimidating or hostile acts directed at a co-worker;

- generally abrasive behavior;

- using obscene, abusive, or threatening language or gestures;

- discrediting a co-worker;

- prohibiting due process;

- slander;

- withholding information vital to the co-workers job-performance;

- acts of physical isolation.

These guidelines are fundamental in nature and are matters of judgment and common sense.

The Organization prohibits mobbing. Any violation of the Organization's anti-mobbing policy should be reported immediately to either your supervisor, the office manager, Human Resources, or the President.

All complaints will be treated confidentially to the maximum extent possible and will be promptly investigated.

The Organization prohibits any form of retaliation against an employee filing a bona fide complaint under this policy or for assisting in a complaint investigation. If the result of the investigation indicates that corrective action is called for, such action may include disciplinary measures up to and including immediate termination of the employment of the offender(s), when the Organization believes, in its sole discretion, such action is warranted.[3]

Risk Assessment

In recent years, increased attention has been focused on behavioral risk assessment and management. Although the definition of mobbing may be as yet unknown to behavioral risks consultants, the symptoms and results of the syndrome are not.[4]

Conflict Management Procedures

Strategies that allow for conflict resolution and mediation can be put into place so that the person who thinks that s/he is a victim has recourse. If the company has no established internal mechanisms, a consultant or a local mediation center can be contacted. Examples of conflict resolution procedures are in Chapter 7.

SYSTEMS THAT ALREADY EXIST
AND PROVIDE GOOD EXAMPLES

Swedish National Board of
Occupational Safety and Health
A Psychologically Safe Environment

In the statute booklet on *Victimization at Work*, available in English, the Swedish National Board of Occupational Safety and Health provides examples of general measures employers can take for prevention. The statute states that attitudes involved in such offensive acts are characterized by a gross lack of respect and offend general principles of honorable and moral behavior. These actions have a negative effect, both short and long term, on individuals and entire working groups. The Board's example follows:[5]

1. A Work Environment Policy which declares the employer's general aims, intentions and attitude toward employees.

2. Procedures that ensure good psychological and social work environments.

3. Steps to prevent people from encountering a negative response at work, e.g., by creating norms which encourage a friendly and respectful climate at the workplace. The employer and its representatives should set the example.

4. Managerial and supervisory personnel training and guidance concerning labor law, effect of different working conditions, interaction and conflict risks in groups, skills for rapid response to people in situations of stress and crisis.

5. Provide a good introduction to enable the employee to adjust to the working group, including a clear explanation of the rules applying to the workplace.

6. Give each employee the best possible knowledge of the activities and their objectives. Regular information and workplace meetings help achieve this.

7. Give all employees information about and a share in the measures agreed on for the prevention of victimization.

8. Try to ensure that duties have substance and meaning and that the capacity and knowledge of the individual are utilized.

9. Give employees opportunities to improve their knowledge and develop in their jobs. Encourage them to pursue this end.

10. Offensive behavior or treatment can never be accepted no matter who is involved or who is the target.

11. The employer must set the example and never subject an employee to victimization, e.g. through abusive power or any other unacceptable behavior or response such as deliberate insults, hypercritical attitudes, ridicule, unfriendliness, or supervision of the employee without his/her knowledge and with harmful intent.

12. Create a reliable basis for two way dialogue, communication, and a genuine desire to solve problems.

Levi Strauss & Co.—A Proactive Approach

Levi Strauss & Co. has an exemplary philosophy. The company has the reputation of being a great place to work. These are their standards:

Teamwork and Trust: Leadership that exemplifies directness, openness to influence, commitment to success of others, willingness to acknowledge our own contributions to problems, personal accountability, teamwork and trust. Not only must we model these behaviors, but we must coach others to adopt them.

Diversity: Leadership that values a diverse workforce (age, sex, ethnic group, etc.) at all levels of the organization, diversity in experience, and a diversity in perspectives. We have committed to taking full advantage of the rich backgrounds and abilities of all our people and to promote a greater diversity in positions of influence. Differing points of view will be sought. Diversity will be valued and honesty rewarded, not suppressed.

Recognition: Leadership that promotes greater recognition—both financial and psychological—for individuals and teams that contribute to our success. Recognition must be given to all who contribute: those who create and innovate and also those who continually support the day-to day business requirements.

Ethical Management Practices: Leadership that epitomizes the stated standards of ethical behavior. We must provide clarity about our expectations and must enforce these standards throughout the corporation.

Communication: Leadership that is clear about Company, unit, and individual goals and performance. People must know what is expected of them and receive timely, honest feedback on their performance and career aspirations.

Empowerment: Leadership that increases the authority and responsibility of those closest to our products and customers. By actively pushing responsibility, trust and recognition into the organization, we can harness and release the capabilities of all our people.[6]

Levi Strauss & Co. has a mission statement and an aspiration statement that are relevant with respect to how the company espouses to treat its employees. We quote excerpts from:

Mission Statement of Levi Strauss & Co.

We will conduct our business ethically and demonstrate leadership in satisfying our responsibilities to our communities and to society. Our work environment will be safe and productive and characterized by fair treatment, teamwork, open communications, personal accountability and opportunities for growth and development.

Levi Strauss & Co. Aspiration Statement (excerpt)

We all want a Company that our people are proud of and committed to, where all the employees have an opportunity to contribute, learn, grow and advance based on merit, not politics or background. We want our people to feel respected, treated fairly, listened to and involved. Above all we want satisfaction from accomplishments and friendships, balanced personal and professional lives, and to have fun in our endeavors.[7]

We interviewed the personnel policy planner from Levi Strauss, Robin Winburn, to ask how this company would address the type of behaviors characteristic of the mobbing syndrome.

ND: *Would you consider jealousy, taking away responsibility, putting rumors into circulation, etc., as harassment?*

RW: *You mean, when a superior uses his or her power to diminish an employee when they are jealous of their accomplishments?*

ND: *Yes.*

RW: *In that case, what we do is use other tools. Not our "No Harassment" policy, but we go to our "Principles of Behavior," that we call our "Aspiration Statement". It talks about the expected standard of behavior to which you are being held accountable. The person that you are talking about would be violating a number of these standards. We are expected to express these standards, or we are subject to discipline.*

ND: *What sanctions do you use?*

RW: *There are a couple of things short of discipline. We have our performance review process which is mid-year and at the end of the year. If there are problems at other times, they are dealt with on a one-to-one basis.*

The discipline process is not a policy but a practice. We call it Performance Improvement Counseling. It has several steps. The process should be fair and consistent.

Employees should be treated with dignity, respect and compassion. You have to balance the interests of the company with the interests of the employee. The employees should receive direct, honest, and timely feedback. I am not saying that we are perfect. These are the written guidelines.

ND: *Your mission statement impressed me. It says: "Our employees' lives are just as important as the quality of the product." Would you stay that this is a valid, living, philosophy in the company?*

RW: *Yes I would. It is certainly one we struggle with. We call it the work-life balance, or work-family balance. We embrace it in principle, various managers express it depending on their own commitment. It is acknowledged that to invoke it is valid.*

We also have a conflict resolution policy. Conflict resolution should reflect our company's aspirations. It should contribute to maintaining a healthy and productive work environment. In a way, it restates our aspirations.

Employees are encouraged to be open, to react in a timely fashion. It does acknowledge that sometimes for some conflicts, like harassment, direct resolution is ineffective. Then we encourage our employees to go to someone else, like human resources. We also have an employee assistance program. So we acknowledge the fact that sometimes you cannot address the conflict.[8]

In early 1999, Levi Strauss & Co. announced that it had to close half of its North American plants and lay off some 5,900 workers. More work would go overseas. There, as we said earlier, often are business decisions that even model companies cannot avoid. But, true to its tradition of treating workers well, Levi Strauss & Co.'s termination package includes extended health benefits, severance pay, and a special fund from which terminated employees can draw for retraining or even for starting up their own small business. And, we want to add, Levi Strauss & Co. also has a code of conduct for its network of subcontractors around the globe.[9]

Saturn Corporation—Respecting All Employees

The principles of the Saturn Corporation illustrate ideal goals and may inspire other organizations. Saturn's philosophy states:

> We believe that all people want to be involved in decisions that affect them, care about their job and each other, take pride in themselves and in their contributions, and share in the success of their effort.

> By creating an atmosphere of mutual trust and respect, recognizing and utilizing individual expertise and knowledge in innovative ways, providing the technologies and education for each individual, we will enjoy a successful relationship and a sense of belonging to an integrated business system capable of achieving our common goals which insures security for our people and success for our business and communities.[10]

Saturn's values on which all behaviors can be measured are:

- Commitment to Customer Enthusiasm
- Commitment to Excel
- Trust and Respect for Each Other
- Teamwork
- Continuous Improvement

These shared values must be fundamental to all Saturn Team Members. Our behavior must support Saturn's values and discourage actions contrary to these shared values. Saturn Team Members must "walk the talk."[11]

INTERVENTION

Disciplinary Actions and Discharge for Severe Misconduct

We believe that mobbing should be defined as severe misconduct, just as would be the case for fraud, theft, gross negligence, physical assault, sexual harassment, etc., and, accordingly, disciplinary action should be initiated.

The Saturn Corporation, often cited as a good example, uses a very comprehensive consultation process for situations which adversely affect members (employees). The process includes counseling, guidance, and review. The purpose is to

- Help, not punish.
- Provide feedback for members.
- Improve team member behavior.

If no improvement can be seen:

Saturn will initiate disciplinary action or discharge when behaviors of team members are contrary to the interest and well-being of all Saturn team members. Such behaviors are in direct violation of Saturn's core values, and are considered by Saturn to constitute severe misconduct.

REHABILITATION

Once the damage has been done, what can management do? Further stigmatizing of the individual must be prevented. Victims must be rehabilitated to their previous reputation and responsibilities. Management may offer:

+ An apology;

+ Therapy;

+ A different position in the company, with training, if necessary;

+ Encouragement and support;

+ Help in finding another job.

In 1987, a Swedish business economist was able to demonstrate that it was less costly for a company to offer employees professional vocational rehabilitation, even a very expensive one, and to reorganize working conditions, than to deal with extended sick leaves, disability claims, or settlements.[12]

IN CONCLUSION—THE BOTTOM LINE

The costs of mobbing to the organization can be very high. The costs of distrust, poor morale, and a diseased corporate culture have a significant impact on any organization's ability to produce and sell a product or service. More expenses incur because of a high turnover rate, recruitment, and new training for the loss of the experience. And last but not least, lawyers' fees, court, and settlement arrangements are a likely hefty expense. But most importantly, what is getting lost is the value of a healthy and humane workplace.

Some organizations will feel they are too busy going about the business at hand to properly address the mobbing syndrome. Others will view a mobbing as a one-time occurrence. For many companies, it can result in chronic problems that debilitate the organization's effectiveness in maintaining its levels of success, or inhibit its growth. And in some cases, it may prove to be fatal to the organization.

Chapter 6 Endnotes

1. *Employee Assistance Program* (EAP) Digest, January/February 1994.

2. Leymann, 1993a.

3. We worded this text for an anti-mobbing policy based on a sample policy against sexual harassment included in Bennett et al., 1998.

4. The CEO of a major East Coast corporation contacted the company's Employee Assistance Program representative to do a corporate culture survey. The company had been experiencing low morale and there had been two suicides on the management level. The CEO, in essence, was asking for a behavioral risk assessment. Incidence quoted from Atkins, Gary L.: Behavioral Risk Management, A New Opportunity for EAP Growth and Development, in *EAPA Exchange* May/June 1997, vol. 27, no. 3, p. 15.

5. AFS, 1993:17, Swedish National Board of Occupational Safety and Health, S-171 84 Solna, Sweden; Tel .+46 8 730 98000, Fax +46 8 730 19 67. Note: The translation has been slightly modified.

6. *Personnel Journal*, 1992:38.

7. *Personnel Journal*, 1992:43.

8. Interview with Robin Winburn, Human Resources Policy Planner, Dec. 24, 1997.

9. *Des Moines Register*, March 2, 1999.

10. The philosophy is stated in the *Memorandum of Agreement* between SATURN and the U.A.W., 1997.

11. From Saturn Corporation, Guiding Principles.

12. Leymann, 1996:174.

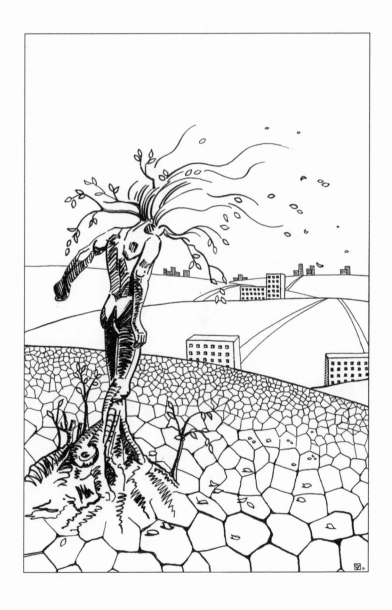

◆ SEVEN ◆

The Challenge of Conflict Resolution

◆

Because conflict resolution is fundamental in helping to avoid a mobbing situation, we explore the nature and dynamics of conflicts in the mobbing context and discuss how things could play out with the appropriate mechanisms in place.

Why do we call this Chapter "The Challenge of Conflict Resolution?" All conflicts can be managed, and at best be resolved, if the parties involved really want to solve the issues. However, in a mobbing, no real attempts are made to understand or resolve the conflict. In a company, with the unspoken rule of "Don't think, don't feel, don't trust, and don't question," as Hall describes such companies,[1] and with no conflict management mechanisms in place, conflict resolution is a futile attempt.

In ideal workplace conditions, with a mature workforce and good leadership, conflicts are handled as learning opportunities. Such organizations have policies and procedures in place to adhere to a conflict resolution process and they have rules of expected conduct. In such a workplace, people are encouraged to find ways to negotiate conflicts in the interest of all concerned, i.e., in the interest of the company as well as in the interest of the employees.

This is what we consider the challenge—or the dilemma. Although conflict resolution can be a simple process it rarely happens when a mobbing occurs. Furthermore, it does not really matter what the conflict is about, whether it is a disagreement over work procedure, a lack of recognition, incivility, harassment, a clash of personalities, or different values. It will, for certain, not happen in organizations that do not have conflict management mechanisms in

157

place and have a culture that avoids dealing with conflict. But if organizations have procedures for conflict resolution and are genuinely interested in a resolution, a mobbing process can most likely be prevented or halted, before it reaches a second or a third degree.

IN THE BEGINNING IS A CONFLICT

Catherine was regarded as a leader in her field and, with some 20 years of management experience, had worked successfully for several years in a responsible staff position in an expanding nonprofit service organization. The culture of the organization had been team-based, self-directed, leaving ample room for initiative and creativity, and was characterized by cordial relations among all staff.

When a new CEO came on board, numerous issues became seemingly unresolvable conflicts for Catherine. Her quotes are an example for *how unresolved conflicts relate to first signs of mobbing.* They also illustrate a first degree mobbing and an early escape.

> Catherine: *Matters over procedures and the nature of work assignments, exclusion from important meetings pertaining to my work area, special assignments concerning my projects given to inexperienced staff, etc., became real conflicts for me. I felt curtailed, controlled, degraded, I felt not trusted. I considered it an assault on my integrity. Was this a power play?*
>
> *I became increasingly confused, depressed, distressed, and actually desperate. I tried to address these issues in a conversation with the CEO. She evaded them and accused me of not being able to deal with change and of being insubordinate.*
>
> *Nothing could have been further from the truth. I was speechless at the time. I had to hold back my tears. I also felt miserable because I was seemingly incapable of resolving the issues. I thought: "I need to be able to fig-*

ure things out, I should be able to find a solution." Only much later did I realize that it was not possible to find a solution.

I now remember the CEO's reaction when I handed her my resignation, three months after she came on board, and explained my reasons for leaving. She did not seem all too surprised and I even detected a sense of relief. Maybe she had prepared herself for a longer haul and was astonished that I resigned so early?

For Catherine, and for all the people in our cases, there is something that bothers them, something that interferes with them accomplishing their task in the best way they know how. They see it as a conflict. They think: "How can we resolve this situation? What can I do? What would be a good solution?" They think and act with good intent to resolve the situation in a constructive way, but they are dealing with individuals who have a predetermined and malevolent intent.

The conflict serves the mobbers' purpose. Their actions are their intent. Their logic is most often determined by the thought: "How can I, or we, get rid of this person?" This is revealed in attacks of various sorts: humiliation, ridicule, stigmatization, ostracism, exclusion, and isolation. All these actions indicate: I/we want you out! That, the targeted individuals do not understand. Initially, they cannot see through the mobbers' game. They are unable to understand and accept the reality early on. This upsets them. They despair. They think: "Am I crazy?" "What is wrong with me?" The feelings of self-doubt escalate and cause confusion, tension, anger, and depression. Sooner or later, the mobbees sense that their attempts at resolving the issues are futile. The conflict goes unresolved.

Unresolved conflicts in mobbing tend to develop a dynamic of their own. They intensify and grow to seemingly unmanageable proportions. One issue escalates into ever more complex issues, mainly through mutual accusations, through action and reaction. Frequently the initial conflict might even be forgotten in the process.

The mobbing cycle has been set into motion. Unresolved conflict contributes to a deterioration of performance, to emotional distress, to temporary and then more frequent absences due to illness. The person's own behavior may now give management or supervisors cause for criticism and induce mobbing behavior.

The more the injured person attempts to find recourse, the more the mobbers create reasons why an issue cannot be resolved. Soon they find enough reasons in the mobbees' behaviors that prove them right. Mutual accusations inflame the situation. When people are unwilling to resolve core issues—and this is the case in a mobbing situation—conflict escalation is an inevitable course of events. The expulsion now becomes only a matter of time.

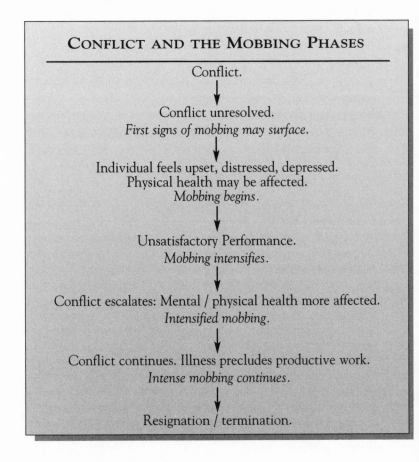

CONFLICT AND THE MOBBING PHASES

Conflict.

↓

Conflict unresolved.
First signs of mobbing may surface.

↓

Individual feels upset, distressed, depressed.
Physical health may be affected.
Mobbing begins.

↓

Unsatisfactory Performance.
Mobbing intensifies.

↓

Conflict escalates: Mental / physical health more affected.
Intensified mobbing.

↓

Conflict continues. Illness precludes productive work.
Intense mobbing continues.

↓

Resignation / termination.

Understanding this process may help mobbees to act, consciously, on a number of choices. It is important that victims understand their choices as early as possible. It might help them break the mobbing cycle before it breaks them. They might understand that they need not be sucked into a destructive game. If they understand that the issues will not get resolved, no matter what, and that they are not at fault, perhaps they will not fall into despair.

A CLASH OF VALUES AND PERSONALITIES

When organizational objectives or values change, very invested and dedicated individuals may no longer identify with the company. It is difficult to compromise their values and beliefs. The more they attempt to stand up for what they consider just and right, the more the mobbing intensifies. What happens then is that they may be seen as not being able to accept change. Not flexible. This often heard accusation is true and false at the same time. Change as such is not the problem. Different values are.

Catherine: *It felt like the ideals and mission of the organization were no longer important. The new CEO actually never answered the question of where she wanted to go. I had chosen to work for the organization because its mission was in line with my beliefs. And what I saw happening, I could not really support.*

John, a dedicated dentist who worked in a state institution for mentally retarded persons: *I had seen all 600 patients in the first six months. As I continued to see everyone every six months, everybody was given some type of treatment. By the end of three years I had developed dental care plans. This was the first time in the institution's history the patients received such thorough care.*

Later, all this lost its importance. Patients were really not able to make any decisions, and the new philosophy was that the patients were in fact responsible for their whole life. It was a severe disagreement with respect to the treatment of patients, over the interpretation of the federal laws. And that happened because the institution was afraid of losing money. With the new mentality, less attention was given to dental matters. Mentally retarded patients do not brush their teeth. They can go for days without brushing their teeth. It is something that needs supervision. If a patient needed treatment on Friday, they would not schedule him, but wait. And then on Saturday, when he had an increased problem, that then became my problem.

Catherine's and John's quotes illustrate a change in interpreting the organization's mission. For those who are highly aligned with the organization and with their professional ethos, a drastic change may signal "betrayal." Their attempt to realign the organization with its original goal or mission may be viewed as undermining change. A clash of values becomes a triggering event.

A clash of personalities can also come about when individuals are motivated by power hunger and ego needs. When organizational goals are subjected to those personal needs, the organization and its people are jeopardized. Employees who sense such insincerity may then be eliminated through mobbing.

UNDERSTANDING CONFLICTS

We said earlier that in a mobbing situation, conflicts are not resolved. Yet, to be able to break the mobbing cycle, it is helpful to better understand the nature of conflicts and what conditions are necessary for a constructive resolution.

Conflicts are a natural part of every relationship. We cannot deny their existence. We can only accept and attempt to understand them. Be guided by them. Deal with them.

All individuals perceive every situation from their own unique perspective. Every human interaction, therefore, contains potential conflict.

People are often bewildered and confused when conflict arises, because they have not learned how to reconcile differences constructively. In a group, be it family, a workplace, or a community, people attempt to minimize differences by focusing on an overall goal, a legal framework, a common belief system, a "culture" that they share and that unifies them.

Managing and resolving conflicts are possible with open, honest, and clear communication that follows a given process. The how-to-resolve-conflict literature abounds and many companies and private consultants offer training courses in this area. It is also encouraging that all across the U.S., and increasingly abroad, programs teach students from K-12th grade conflict management skills, including how to deal with bullies and how not to assume bullying behaviors. In the U.S., information on what is happening in any state can be obtained through The Conflict Resolution Education Network (CREnet).[2]

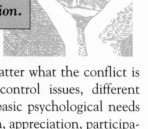

With mobbing, the existing conflicts are not really dealt with because the goal becomes the elimination of the person from the workplace. This precludes a true negotiated resolution.

As we said earlier, it does not really matter what the conflict is about—procedures, a personality clash, control issues, different values, or change. What matters is, that basic psychological needs have not been honored, such as recognition, appreciation, participation, respect, autonomy.

In Catherine's case, it was not the fact that a new CEO took over. It was not so much the particular changes in procedures that were established that affected her sense of self. What she was deeply troubled by was that her responsibilities were curtailed and she was excluded from participation in decisions. She needed to be treated as a competent, self-directed, valuable and participating member of a team, and not as an incompetent individual that required controlling.

WAYS OF HANDLING CONFLICTS
YOU HAVE CHOICES

Before approaching a person with whom one has a conflict, it is help-ful to analyze and understand one's own feelings and motives as clearly as possible, as well as attempting to understand the other per-son's feelings and motives. Asking questions like: "Why do I feel this way? What is it that I really want? Why am I so upset by this? Why do the mobbers act the way they do?" helps one not to be controlled by one's feelings but to stand back and examine the situation.

It is a process that directs a person out of confusion onto a clear-er path. This is a position of strength. Persons who find themselves in a mobbing situation may need assistance from others to help them analyze this more clearly. They may be too hurt and upset by the attacks they have suffered to go through this process unguided.

There are five ways to handle a conflict: avoiding or living with it, giving in, imposing one's way, compromising, and working things out to everybody's satisfaction. Which approach individuals choose depends on different factors: their character and experiences; how they have learned to deal with conflict; the particular circumstances; the type of conflict; its importance for the person; in what way they relate to the other person, or how they predict the other person will react.

It may be helpful to point out that, generally, men and women have different resolution styles. Women, more often than not, want to discuss the issues and work them out cooperatively. For men, con-flict in itself becomes a competition. As we know now, from studies done by John Gray and Deborah Tannen, men fear loss of status, whereas women in a conflict often fear the loss of relationship. Not dealing with conflicts directly, then, often stems from those particu-lar fears.[3]

In any case, conflict resolution that honors all parties is only possible if the individuals involved genuinely want to find solutions. In a mobbing, people will resort to the power of their position, or to their evil intent, to get things done their way, irrespective of the employees' wishes, possibilities, viewpoints, wants, or needs. Therein lies the challenge for the injured party to realize that conflict resolution may not be possible.

> Catherine: *I did not realize at the time that the disagreements about my work assignments were not disagreements. They actually were power plays and part of a plan to force me out. Consequently, my attempts to have a constructive dialogue ended in despair. I did not understand. Not then. The only solution that I saw was to get out. As quickly as possible.*

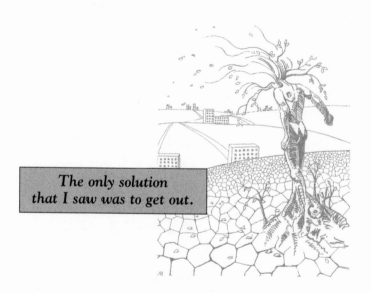

The only solution that I saw was to get out.

Would it have been a solution if Catherine had just subjected herself to whatever her new boss wanted from her, by just giving in, assuming an inferior role, not living up to her capabilities and her strength? Perhaps, but the costs would have been compromising her own ideals. Others, like Neil, are better able to shield themselves and for a longer period of time.

People, who have become mobbing targets cannot be saved from the painful experience of an emotionally unhealthy work environment. But they can be saved from the self-doubt that leads to depression and illness, or from feelings of revenge.

With that realization, they might have the strength to prepare and seek employment elsewhere. It would mean leaving a work environment that is detrimental to their health to work in a nourishing environment that hopefully values and appreciates them.

When victims see the mobbing situation at their workplace for what it is, they might gain strength from this insight. They can gain some distance and muster their forces and strength to stick it out a few more weeks or months while preparing for a transition. They can gain inner strength and act on the conviction that they will find another opportunity. It is always easier to find another job while still on the job. They might need the help of family and friends and a therapist. But they will understand that they worked in an unhealthy environment, that it is not their fault, and that they need to find a healthy one if they want to survive.

In any event, what are your options when you find yourself in a mobbing environment? What can you do when no structural avenues are open and no one seems to want to listen? Earlier we listed some options:

1. *Stay on and hold on.* Possible course of events: Illness, prolonged sick leave, more conflicts, eventual forced resignation or termination. In severe depression, suicide has been a choice as well.

2. *Emotional, inner resignation.* Emotional or inner resignation is a temporary, practical change of attitude, of distancing yourself from your personal investment in the job. By directing emotional energies on activities outside of the job, such as hobbies, family, or other work you can gain distance, perspective, and even joy.

3. *Escape.* Separation by resignation. Leaving the job and escaping to a different and healthy environment.

4.   *Bring legal action* as an attempt to gain financial
      redress and justice.

In the course of events, you may choose more than one of these options. Catherine escaped early on. Diana decided to leave and bring legal action that ended in a settlement. Joan's company offered a settlement to avoid her taking legal action. Judy escaped and found another job. Neil and Robert, as we saw in Chapter 4, decided to hold on, because they felt strong enough and had developed some survival mechanisms.

A postscript to Catherine's story. Catherine's boss, after one year, was asked to resign. The reasons for the board's decision have not been made public.

POSSIBLE SOLUTIONS FOR ORGANIZATIONS

It is the culture of the organization that determines whether potential mobbing behavior has a chance to escalate or is being curtailed at any one point in the cycle. There are many different ways of actually addressing a conflict when it arises. Any organization or company, no matter how small or what it does, can have mechanisms and policies in place that fit their specific culture. The following structural strategies for conflict management can help to halt mobbing early on or bring redress to the injured party.

1.   Create an open door policy.

2.   Create company procedures. A good example are the
      conflict resolution procedures adopted by Saturn
      Corporation, see Box.

3.   Train selected employees, or better still, all
      employees, in conflict management and/or
      mediation.

4.   Establish a mediation center within the
      organization.[4]

5. Contract with an outside mediator/ombudsperson on a retainer basis, so confidentially can be maintained.

6. Contract with a mediation center in your community.

7. Have a professional mediator on staff, just as companies also have lawyers or medical personnel on staff.

Generally, employees feel most valued and are more productive if they can work cooperatively, in teams, as self-directed as possible, where they feel trusted, where they can be honest, and where their creativity is valued.

SATURN'S CONFLICT RESOLUTION PROCEDURES[5]

The philosophy and mission of Saturn and the roles and responsibilities of all concerned stress the need for decision making and problem solving at the most appropriate level of the organization.

STEP 1

Should members encounter problems in the Work Unit relationship, the Work Unit members will attempt to solve the problems, with the assistance and cooperation of the Work Unit Counselor and Operation Module Advisors (OMA), where appropriate. In those rare instances where Work Unit problems cannot be resolved, the matter will be referred to the next step.

STEP 2

The OMA will notify and discuss the issue with the member and the Crew Coordinator or Skilled Trades Advisor. The Crew Coordinator or Skilled Trades Advisors will seek resolution of the issue, which will include informing and discussing the issue with the Business Unit People Systems Advisor where appropriate.

If unresolved the issue shall be reduced to writing on a form with a heading "Member Conflict Form" which will be signed by the member and presented to the Business Unit People Systems Advisor by the Crew Coordinator or Skilled Trades Advisor. Thereafter, a meeting will be scheduled within seven working days between the Crew Coordinator or Skilled Trades Advisor and the Business Unit Advisor, and the Business Unit People Systems Advisor to stipulate the agreed to facts, and seek resolution of the issue.

STEP 3

If unresolved within 14 working days of the agreed to statement of facts, the issue will be reviewed in a meeting of all Advisors. The consensus technique will be utilized in the effort to resolve the issue. Minutes from the meeting will be issued within seven working days. If unresolved, an appeal must be made within seven working days, using a form supplied by Saturn, to the Vice President of People Systems stating their desire to appeal the conflict. Both parties will exchange statements within 14 working days from the date of the appeal.

Any conflict not appealed by the Regional Director within 30 days will be considered settled on the basis of the last answer. The Conflict will then be reviewed at an appeal meeting by the Vice President of People Systems for Saturn and the International Union. If consensus resolution is not reached, Saturn and the Union will exchange final statements within 14 working days following the meeting.

STEP 4

The issue may be appealed to an impartial Umpire if unresolved at Step 3. The Regional Director or GM Department may submit an appeal for the Umpire within 21 working days of the final exchange of statements or the issue will be considered settled on the basis of the last written answer. If appealed, the issue will be referred for final and binding decision by the Umpire. The parties will share the cost of the impartial Umpire on a 50/50 basis.

Note: Time limits can be extended by mutual agreement at any step of the procedure.

Chapter 7 Endnotes

1. Hall, 1991:55

2. CREnet merged with ACR (Association for Conflict Resolution, www.acresolution.org). 1527 New Hampshire Avenue, NW, Washington DC 20036, Tel. 202-667-9700, FAX 202-665-1968, <www.crenet.org>.

3. John Gray, *Men Are from Mars and Women Are from Venus*; Deborah Tannen, *You Just Don't Understand; and Talking from 9-5*.

4. There are several universities with a mediation center on campus for staff, students and faculty.

5. Saturn Member Conflict Resolution Procedure, In: *Guiding Principles*, pages 36-37. We slightly altered the text, mainly by deleting company-specific abbreviations. We thank Saturn Corporation for granting permission to reproduce these Conflict Resolution Procedure.

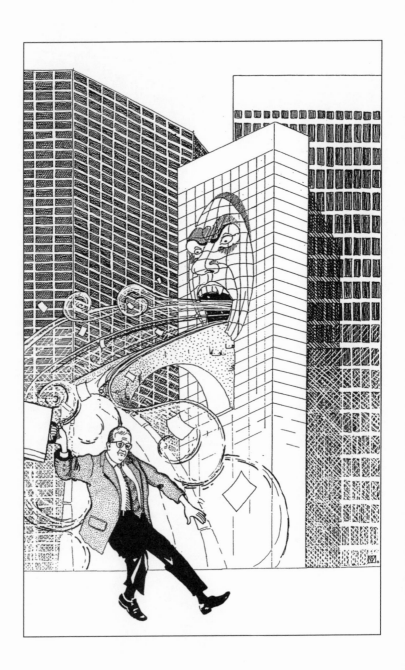

◆ EIGHT ◆

Mobbing and the Law*

When injuries result from worksite exposure to chemical substances, the offending institutions are compelled to introduce remedies. When the injuries originate from toxic human behavior, no less should occur.

—Harvey Hornstein
Brutal Bosses and Their Prey

◆

In this Chapter we speak to mobbing victims about rights they have in existing laws. We alert employers to these rights and urge them to prohibit mobbing behavior in their organizations or risk legal action and financial loss. And we appeal to lawmakers to develop new legislation—an anti-mobbing law—that will more explicitly cover the abuses inflicted on victims of mobbing.

PRESENT RIGHTS AND STATUTES

We wish to emphasize that mobbing is a new cause of action, and a need for anti-mobbing legislation is paramount, as has been long recognized in some European countries. Although "mobbing" per se is not covered under present laws in any of the 50 U.S. states, there are

---

Our key reference for this chapter is _Employment Relationships: Law and Practice_ by Mark W. Bennett, Donald J. Polden, and Howard J. Rubin, Aspen Publishers, Inc.,1998. This chapter is in no way a substitute for the services of an attorney. We have neither liability nor responsibility to any person or entity.

For practical considerations addressing legal redress, see Chapter 4, How You Can Cope.

laws that have been used successfully to argue the mobbing victim's case, particularly civil rights laws. The following discusses some rights and statutes that may pertain to your case.

CIVIL RIGHTS LEGISLATION

Most American workers believe they have some protection as an employee because of our country's civil rights laws. However, nearly all of us are unclear about the specifics of these laws. Beginning with *Title VII of the Civil Rights Act of 1964*, it became "an unlawful employment practice for an employer. . .to discharge any individual, or otherwise to discriminate against any individual with respect to his compensation, terms, conditions, or privileges of employment, because of such individual's race, color, religion, sex, or national origin." [1]

Later federal and state acts, including *The Age Discrimination in Employment Act of 1967*, *The Vocational Rehabilitation Act of 1973*, and *The Americans with Disabilities Act of 1990*, protected age, pregnancy, and disability. Although there is presently no explicit federal statute protection for sexual orientation, several states include this protection in their employment discrimination statutes. In *Oncale v. Sundowner* (1998), the Supreme Court held that same-sex harassment can be actionable under Title VII.

In the most recent legislation, *The Civil Rights Act of 1991*, major changes were implemented that expanded existing federal anti-discrimination laws and overruled previous court decisions that had limited employees' legal recourse.

Your particular mobbing complaint may fall under one of these laws because of your *protected status*. For example, you believe you have been mobbed because of your age. Since there is no specific legislation at this time regarding mobbing, you decide to file a claim under the Civil Rights protection against age discrimination. In order to proceed with your complaint, you will need to file a claim with your state's Civil Rights Commission and the Federal Equal Employment Opportunity Commission (EEOC).

Also, at this time you may decide to seek legal counsel. However you proceed, make certain you follow the time frames allowed in the Civil Rights laws or you may lose your opportunity to file a case.

HOSTILE ENVIRONMENT

The Supreme Court has found that Title VII is not limited to economic or tangible discrimination but is also intended to protect people from having to work in a hostile or abusive environment. Title VII is violated when the workplace is permeated with intimidation, ridicule, and insult which alter the conditions of the victim's employment.

The claim of a "hostile environment" has often been used in the context of sexual harassment and other Title VII cases. In mobbing cases, however, a hostile workplace environment is often based on *general* (nonsexual/nonracial) *harassment*. Because the mobbee always experiences a hostile environment, as defined under Title VII, we believe it is a strong argument in mobbing claims.

The Supreme Court further identified the following factors to be considered in determining a hostile environment:

1. Frequency of the conduct;

2. Its severity;

3. Whether it is physically threatening or humiliating or a mere offensive utterance;

4. Whether it unreasonably interferes with an employee's work performance.[2]

We have previously noted these as prevalent in workplace mobbing.

The Supreme Court also concluded:

1. This conduct must create an environment that is sufficiently severe or pervasive that a *reasonable person* would find it hostile or abusive; and

2. The victim subjectively perceives the environment to be abusive.[3]

Whether used as an expanded interpretation of Title VII or a new law, this clarification of what defines a hostile work environment should constitute clear protection for mobbing victims.

Voluntary Resignation or Constructive Discharge?

"Constructive discharge" occurs when an employer intentionally renders working conditions so intolerable that an employee is essentially forced to leave the employment. . .The working conditions are deemed intolerable if a reasonable employee would find them to be so.[4]

To have a good cause for your defense, you must have "resigned," but be able to demonstrate that you were, in fact, "constructively discharged." Some circuit courts of appeal have treated "constructive discharge" as proof that the employee's resignation was not really voluntary.

Retaliatory Discharge—Protection to File a Claim

If you assert a claim against your employer under Title VII and your employer responds by terminating you, you may have a claim of retaliation. This protection should also extend to mobbing victims.

TORTS RELATING TO ACTS OF MOBBING

Torts are wrongful acts resulting in injury to another's person, property, or reputation for which the injured party is entitled to seek redress. The following torts may apply to mobbing victims.

Intentional Infliction of Emotional Distress

Because of the grave mental injury inflicted on mobbing victims, the tort of *intentional infliction of emotional distress* should offer a mobbing victim another basis for legal action. This argument must prove that the conduct was extreme, severe, enduring and/or outrageous.

> Liability has been found only where the conduct has been so outrageous in character, and so extreme in degree, as to go beyond all possible bounds of decency, and to be regarded as atrocious, and utterly intolerable in a civilized community.

> Generally, the case is one in which the recitation of the facts to an average member of the community would arouse his resentment against the actor, and lead him to exclaim, "Outrageous!" [5]

As seen from our interview partners and the mobbing literature, victims suffer such severe distress, caused by cumulative outrageous behaviors, that depression, panic attacks, and even strokes or heart attacks are linked to workplace mobbing.

Bennett et al., state: "Although severe emotional distress is often accompanied by some physical and bodily harm, the rule is not limited to such cases. Where the *conduct is sufficiently extreme and outrageous, there may be liability for emotional distress alone.*" [6]

However, Professor David Yamada cautions, "I wish to emphasize that many Intentional Infliction of Emotional Distress claims in workplace settings lose because the courts find that the behavior in question was not severe and outrageous. Some very serious instances of mobbing/bullying go unpunished as a result."

Yamada continues, "Also, some courts have held that workers' compensation provides the "exclusive remedy" for work-induced stress. Therefore intentional infliction of emotional distress claims may not be brought in such situations." [7]

Defamation—Libel/Slander Statements

Defamation may have relevance in your mobbing case. Defamation includes dissemination of false information to a third party, usually other employees, clients or customers, or prospective employers, which injures the person's reputation and questions his or her skills.

Written defamatory statements constitute *libel*, whereas oral defamatory statements are *slander*. As an example, in 1991, *Lutz v. Royal Insurance Company*, the court noted the following.

> A false statement is defamatory if it exposes a person to hatred, contempt or ridicule, or subjects him to a loss of good will and confidence of others, or so harms his reputation, as to deter others from associating with him.[8]

Although you must provide proof that the libel or slander has no merit in fact, some courts have found defamatory those statements which merely *imply* incompetence or inability to perform.

THE AT-WILL DOCTRINE, CONTRACTS, AND PUBLIC POLICY

Because most states are employment at-will states, often cited is the *employer's right to terminate an employee at will*. Employees, and many employers, interpret this to mean the employee can be terminated for *no cause*.

However, all employment is an agreement or contract between the employer and the employee and there are certain rights you do have, regardless of the at-will doctrine or whether or not you have a written contract.

A written agreement that sets down the terms of employment is usually considered preferable. However, you may have only an oral agreement, or even unstated assumptions, based on one or more conversations with your employer, that state you can only be terminated for "just cause."

In a few cases, employees may have rights under one of the following.

1. *Express* contract limitations. This is an expressed (written) agreement that alters the terms of the at-will relationship by laying out in writing your specific agreement.

2. *Implied-in-fact* contract limitations. An example is an employer's promise not to fire an employee except for just cause. This is often found in the policy manual.

3. *Implied-in-law* contract limitations. An example is the implied covenant of "good faith and fair dealing," which imposes upon both parties to the contract "that neither do anything that might have the effect of destroying or injuring the right of the other to receive the fruits of the contract."[9]

Employment-At-Will Rule

The *at-will rule* is more than 100 years old and was originally written by the Tennessee Supreme Court in *Payne v. Western Atlantic R.R.* as the following:

> Men must be left, without interference, to buy and sell where they please, and to discharge or retain employees at will for good cause or for no cause, or even for bad cause without thereby being guilty of an unlawful act per se. It is a right which an employee may exercise in the same way, to the same extent, for the same cause or want of cause as the employer.[10]

However, in recent court decisions the rule is often stated:

> Unless an employment contract expressly specifies a term of employment, an employer may discharge an employee for a good cause, a bad cause, or no cause at all, that is not contrary to law.

That is not contrary to law recognizes that exceptions, as well as state or federal anti-discrimination laws, *may prohibit certain reasons for dismissal regardless of at-will employment.*[11]

Wrongful Discharge in Violation of Public Policy

The most widely recognized exception to at-will employment is wrongful discharge in violation of public policy. This generally prohibits two kinds of terminations—abusive and retaliatory.

Abusive discharge is motivated by the *employer's* animus (hostility, strong hatred) towards the employee because of the employee's status or knowledge. A court ruled abusive discharge where the employee's termination "was motivated solely by [the employer's] desire. . .to conceal improprieties and illegal activities which plaintiff might have disclosed." This cause of action was based on the employee's knowledge of the employer's improprieties.

Another case recognized as "abusive discharge in violation of public policy" was where the employer's motivation was the *employee's status*—race, color, religion, marital status, etc.

Retaliatory discharge is motivated by the *employee's conduct*. In such cases, an employee has been discharged because s/he:

a. Refused to commit an illegal act, such as perjury;

b. Performed a public duty or obligation, such as serving on a jury;

c. Exercised a legal right or privilege, such as filing a workers' compensation claim;

d. Reported the misconduct of an employer or co-employee—"whistle-blowing."

In the court case of *Thompto v. Coborn's Incorporated*, Nov. 23, 1994, the former employee sued her employer for discrimination, breach of contract, and tortuous conduct, based upon the termination of her employment. When the former employer moved for a summary judgment, the judge ruled:

1. Iowa public policy precluded the termination of the employee for inquiring about cancer insurance coverage and requesting information for why coverage was not available;

2. Iowa public policy precluded termination of employee for threatening to consult with attorney to obtain such coverage or explanation;

3. Employer's conduct was sufficiently outrageous to support claim for intentional infliction of emotional distress;

4. Qualified privilege enjoyed by employer with regard to defamation claim extended to self-publication by employee.[12]

It is important to note that in some jurisdictions, the employee's at-will status may heighten the required outrageousness. In other courts, the focus may shift from the reasons for discharge to the manner in which the discharge was carried out. This may be especially relevant to arguing mobbing cases.

WORKERS' COMPENSATION
NONTRAUMATIC MENTAL INJURIES
MENTAL-MENTAL

Another cause for action for victims of mobbing may fall under mental injury suffered on the job. Several states including Arizona, California, Iowa, Wisconsin, and Wyoming have enacted rules and regulations that acknowledge the mental injury that workers can suffer on the job as a result of mental stimuli or stress. These types of injuries are called nontraumatic mental injuries and are referred to as *mental-mental injury.*

Legislatures in those states have passed laws stating that mental illness, with no accompanying physical ailment, such as a back injury, may be considered for compensation as a cumulative effect caused by work-related stress. Through workers' compensation insurance, such injuries can be compensated and damage claimed.

An example of this is the Francis C. Dunlavey case. This case became noteworthy when Francis Dunlavey was awarded a workers' compensation claim in 1996 based on a decision by the Iowa Supreme Court.

The court ruled that Dunlavey should receive compensation for a *mental-mental injury.* All of the physicians giving an opinion in this case agreed that the claimant's work environment was the major cause of his depression. Under previous Workers' Compensation claims, employees have been awarded compensation for mental illness only when a result of the physical injury on the job.

This is the first case in Iowa which established that *mental-mental injury* is compensable if, after proving medical causation, the employee establishes that mental injury was caused by work stress of greater magnitude than day-to-day mental stresses experienced by other workers employed in same or similar jobs, regardless of employer.[14]

WORKPLACE PROTECTION STATUTES OCCUPATIONAL SAFETY AND HEALTH ACT—OSHA

Although occupational safety and health regulations do not expressly include psychological and emotional safety, the statutes that regulate workplace safety can be interpreted as an intent by legislatures to protect employees from any type of injury or victimization.

For this reason, we believe that mobbing should be covered by workplace safety rules and regulations, particularly pertaining to preventive measures in the context of occupational safety and health. We propose that anti-mobbing rules should be included in future OSHA regulations, as has been realized in other countries, particularly in Sweden.

At present, a specific OSHA standard has not been adopted covering *psychological or emotional hazards* in the workplace. However, the "general duty clause" contained in Iowa Code Section 88.4, allows OSHA to cite and penalize for workplace health and safety hazards that are not covered by a specific OSHA standard, but only if they cause or are likely to cause physical harm.

PROCEDURAL CONSIDERATIONS

Timing—When Should You File Your Claim?

Presently, the time limits for bringing discrimination claims are very short, often as little as six months or 180 days after the last act of harassment or discrimination. If you miss the deadline, even by one day, your claim is dismissed. Therefore, it is important to discuss your legal concerns with a qualified attorney or the appropriate civil rights enforcement agency, such as the EEOC, as soon as possible.

Individual Liability vs Employer Liability

Whom should you file a claim against, the individuals who are involved in the mobbing, or the organization? Under Title VII, the majority of discrimination cases that have been appealed have found that individual employees cannot be held liable.

Employers have been held responsible for acts of individuals who serve in a supervisory position and exercise significant control over hiring, firing, or conditions of employment. Other issues considered have included whether the employer provided reasonable avenues for complaint, and whether the employer knew of the conduct but did nothing about it.

Because of this, the claim is usually filed against the employer.

Payment of Damages

The humiliation, wounded pride, anger, hurt, frustration, discomfort, and mental anguish caused by mobbing should be considered emotional harm that justifies, by standards of fairness, emotional distress payments. An amount of compensatory and punitive damages for the emotional pain and future financial losses should be established.

APPEAL TO LAWMAKERS

. . . all of the weapons in the federal statutory arsenal should be viewed . . . as examples of Congress's concerted effort to protect employees from all forms of workplace abuse.

—Mark Bennett, Donald Polden, Howard Rubin
Employment Relationships:Law and Practice

Mobbing as emotional assault in the American workplace has not yet been recognized as a separate cause of action. Consequently, there are no laws that explicitly deal with this type of injury.

Victims of mobbing are insufficiently protected, even though mobbing cases could be dealt with under a number of different legal arguments, especially under "protected status" where applicable. However, since mobbing can happen to anyone, individuals should not need to be identified as members of a specific class to receive protection.

We, therefore, urge lawmakers, because of the prevalence of workplace mobbing and its traumatic nature, to consider new legislation that:

1. Specifies the circumstances of mobbing;

2. Recognizes the grave emotional and physical illnesses that ensue;

3. Serves as a preventive instrument; and

4. Constitutes a better protection for potential victims.

New content needs to be developed to shape legal concepts that protect victims and compensates the harm inflicted on them.

Chapter 8 Endnotes

1. Bennett, et al., 1998:4.02 [A] 4-8.

2. Bennett, et al., 1998:4.02 [A] 4-17.

3. Bennett, et al., 1998:4.02 [A] 4-18.

4. Bennett, et al., 1998:4.02 [C] 4-84.

5. Bennett, et al., 1998:8.05 [A] 4-64.

6. Bennett et. al., 1998:8.05 [B] 8-70.

7. David Yamada, personal communication, 3/30/99.

8. Bennett, et al., 1998:8.02 [B] 8-8.

9. Bennett, et al., 1998:2.03 [A] 2-21.

10. Bennett, et al., 1998:2.02 [B] 2-4.

11. Bennett, et al., 1998:2.02 [B] 2-4.

12. Thompto v. Coborn's Incorporated 871 F. Supp. 1097 (1994).

13. Bennett, et al., 1998:2.04 [A] 2-38.

14. FRANCIS C. DUNLAVEY, Claimant, v. ECONOMY FIRE AND CASUAL-TY CO., Insurance Carrier, Defendants. File No. 858652 APPEAL DECISION by the Iowa Industrial Commissioner, October 26, 1992. DUNLAVEY v. ECONOMY FIRE AND CASUALTY CO., 526 N.W. 2d 845, 858 (Iowa 1995).

THOUGHTS FROM ONE REVIEWER

Your book stimulated my memory as I absorbed it over the past few days. Since I have personal experience with mobbing, I approached the material from several perspectives.

First, I read as a manager and executive where I reviewed my own behavior when I was in those positions. I asked myself, "Did I participate in the activity of mobbing? Did I support this kind of behavior in others? Did I intervene if and when I observed it?"

I determined that I did not participate nor support mobbing. I did not observe mobbing within my realm. At the same time realizing that I have shared a human tendency to "build a case" against an idea or even a person to support my choices, I see that in myself and others as a means of self-protection. I have felt that way and may not have acted that way.

Second, as an individual who experienced mobbing early in my career as a supervisor, this information was helpful for me to see what was occurring at that time. It is a very distant memory now. However, more recently I was mobbed as an independent consultant. I have a sense of completeness about this latest event because I made responsible choices for myself in concluding those relationships. This was not a pleasant experience. It gave me the opportunity to know, without a doubt, narcissistic personality disorder.

Third, as a sister, I have watched a brother agonize over impossible mobbing on the job. Losing status, demeaned by unannounced work schedule changes, ridiculed by supervisors and managers in front of co-workers, blamed for events that did not occur on his shift, etc. Yet, he stays. Why? He loves the work, he fears being too old to secure a job of comparable salary and benefits, and staying has become a crusade of honor, even if it hurts.

Fourth, as a child, I was shamed by mobbing behaviors towards me within my family. I recognized the experiences of your interview partners as equivalent to much of what I repeatedly faced in my youth.[1]

NINE

Acting on Awareness

..there will be no meaningful change in either the occurrence or consequence of abuse unless the structure of the workplace is reformed according to a new social compact, one that encourages cooperation, justice, and a heightened and broadened sense of community.

—Harvey Hornstein
Brutal Bosses and Their Prey

We must work to uncover and reverse the atrocities, one person, one company, and one law at a time.

—Gary and Ruth Namie
BullyProof Yourself at Work

♦

We emphasized throughout this book that mobbing is essentially a group phenomenon. Yet, to act responsibly, individuals need to strengthen their own awareness of the nature and consequences of the mobbing syndrome and understand the role they may play in perpetuating it. This requires personal vigilance not to be caught in a collective craze. On the opposite page is an example of such careful self-examination.

In the preceding chapters we analyzed the mobbing syndrome and discussed what it is and why it occurs. We described how emotional assaults affect the victimized person, what friends and family can do, what happens in organizations and what precautions can be taken. In this chapter we ask, How does mobbing affect our society as a whole? How can we all—as members of a civil society—help prevent mobbing? The impact on one individual has a negative ripple effect on families, the organization, communities, and the wider society.

Earlier we pointed out the link that exists between mobbing and the tension it causes in personal relationships, sometimes even ending in separation or divorce, not to speak of the harm this causes to children. It creates emotional hardship for everyone involved.

Communities lose the creativity and productivity of the mobbed person who for months and years may be mentally occupied with past events on the job and not free to contribute to society in as meaningful a way as s/he did previously. When mobbing occurs, everyone pays.

The social and economic impact of the mobbing syndrome has yet to be measured in quantitative terms in the United States. There is no research to substantiate these costs. Yet, the Bureau of National Affairs estimated in 1990 that five to six billion dollars annually is lost by real or perceived abuse at the workplace.[2]

To protect the Swedish national budget from heavy financial burdens caused by mobbing, the *Vocational Rehabilitation Act* went into effect in 1994. This law states that employers are obliged to present a vocational rehabilitation plan to the Social Insurance Office as soon as an employee has been on sick leave one month, or ten times within a twelve-month period. The purpose of this enactment is to transfer costs for rehabilitation to the origin: the workplace where the mobbing—the emotional injury—occurred.[3]

Other data from Sweden indicate that highly abused employees tend to request early retirement.[4]

Leymann estimated that some 10-15% of all suicides in Sweden could be attributed to workplace mobbing.[5] Although this is some-what uncertain, as actual data are almost impossible to come by, other researchers have confirmed, that almost half of the victims in their surveys have contemplated suicide.[6]

Currently there are more than 30,000 suicides annually in the U.S., about 12 per 100,000 persons, or 1 suicide every 17 minutes. If we used the conservative Swedish percentage of 10% of all suicides attributable to workplace issues, there would be some 3,000 suicides in the U.S. directly linked to the workplace.[7]

As far as workplace homicide is concerned, employers and employees are killed every year because of arguments over money, property, or other reasons. Every so often, the media inform us of workplace shootings by disgruntled employees, but there is rarely a report that identifies the deeper background of these tragedies. [8]

The following table is a partial list of the psychosocial impact and social costs of mobbing and of the actual financial costs that ensue to the individuals, their families and communities.

PSYCHOSOCIAL AND FINANCIAL COSTS

Impact on	Psychosocial Costs	Financial Costs
INDIVIDUALS	• Stress • Emotional illness • Physical illness • Accidents • Disability • Isolation • Pain of separation • Loss of job-identity • Loss of friendships • Suicide/homicide	• Over the counter medication • Therapy • Doctor bills • Hospital bills • Cost of Accidents • Insurance premiums • Lawyer bills • Unemployment • Underemployment • Job Search • Relocation
FAMILIES	• The pain of feeling helpless • Confusion and conflicts • Pain of separation and/or divorce • Impact on children • The costs of separation or divorce	• Loss of family income • The costs of separation or divorce • Therapy
ORGANIZATIONS	• Dissent • Diseased corporate culture • Poor morale • Curtailed creativity	• Increased use of sick leave • Costs of higher turnover • Lowered productivity • Lowered quality work • Loss of expertise • Workers' compensation payments • Unemployment costs • Legal/settlement costs • Early retirement • Increased personnel management costs
SOCIETY/ COMMUNITY	• Unhappy members of society • Political apathy	• Health care costs • Insurance costs • Loss of taxes due to un- or underemployment • Increased demands on public assistance programs • Increased demands on community mental health programs • Increased demands on disability

Various segments of society can play important roles in helping to prevent mobbing. In the following we address what researchers, the media, the health care industry, help-hotlines, employee assistance programs, insurance agencies, unions, state and federal agencies, educators, organizational consultants, the legal community can do in unison to prevent mobbing from occurring.

RESEARCH
BUILDING A FOUNDATION FOR ACTION

The research on mobbing and bullying was initiated in Scandinavia, from where it moved into other European countries. As yet, very little research on the extent, nature, and costs of mobbing in the workplace has been undertaken in the U.S. Researchers in healthcare, economics, organizational psychology and development, etc., should add important data for proposed action in this country.[9]

THE MEDIA—BUILDING AWARENESS

Change is also fostered by public awareness, and the media are instrumental for creating awareness. Journalists can alert people to the existence of the mobbing syndrome. They can initiate public debate and education.

If you experienced a mobbing situation, you might want to consider sending your story to a newspaper or to a business publication together with a reference to this book. If you know of someone else experiencing what appears to be mobbing, you might want to encourage them to do the same. You will have to weigh the pros and cons of such a step quite carefully, so as not to create more personal harm. However, the more stories are told, the greater the momentum for change.

HEALTH CARE SERVICE—A KEY

Nurses, doctors, and therapists have a crucial role to play. Everyday they deal with people coming to them with stress-related illnesses. As we have stated throughout this book, people who work in a mobbing environment over long periods of time can become very ill. Treating the stress-related illness itself may not be sufficient.

We recommend that healthcare professionals do the following:

1. Find out what is going on at work and whether the cause of the patient's symptoms might indeed come from workplace mobbing.

2. Educate yourself and train colleagues to understand the mobbing syndrome so that they can recognize the cause of the symptoms and can give appropriate advice.

3. Help patients understand the mobbing syndrome.

4. Apply post-traumatic stress treatment protocols to victims of workplace mobbing.

HELP-HOTLINES IN THE COMMUNITY "FIRST RESPONDERS"

Many communities have 24-hour help-hotlines usually operated by social service agencies. In many instances they are staffed by well-trained volunteers. It is essential to further train them about the mobbing syndrome so that they can better understand and give appropriate advice and make referrals.

EMPLOYEE ASSISTANCE PROGRAMS (EAPs) A CRUCIAL ROLE AND A WORD OF CAUTION

Employee Assistance Program (EAP) professionals are often the first to whom an employee with psychosocial problems turns or is referred. They play a crucial role in identifying the cause of the mental health problem and can therefore act quickly and appropriately. Many EAP professionals are especially trained in behavioral risk management. It is therefore indispensable that they become aware of the consequences of mobbing at the workplace as a possible high risk factor for behavioral problems and for the person's feelings of distress, depression, and possibly for their suicidal thoughts. Only by understanding the workplace environment can they offer appropriate help.

Because of their connection to the employer, they may also be in a good position to alert management to what is actually going on in any given organization. However, if management is involved in the mobbing, this becomes a major predicament. EAP professionals protect the rights of the client and thus they should maintain strict confidentiality. However, not all employers endorse the same level of confidentiality. As a client of an EAP, you should ask for a written explanation of your employer's policy regarding confidentiality.[10]

You might want to be cautious for another reason also. Wyatt and Hare, in their book *Work Abuse*, express a warning in requesting the help of EAP professionals as "they are paid to operate from the presupposition that any conflict is your fault, owing to a personal problem you are having or a personality characteristic that you need to change. They will not look at the system in which you work because they do not have permission (or perhaps knowledge) to deal with it." [11]

HEALTH INSURANCE COMPANIES
SOUNDING THE ALARM

Mobbing increases the need for health care. Insurance companies might be alerted to workplace mobbing if increased claims are filed from employees of a particular company or from a particular division within a company.

Behavioral Risk Assessments are a matter of course for insurance agencies to determine premiums. Merely the threat of review may cause organizations to take greater preventive measures against mobbing.

Insurance agencies might also wish to develop informational materials on mobbing for employees as well for the employer to direct greater attention to this problem with the hope of reducing their cost.

UNIONS—ANOTHER KEY

Where unions exist today, they too are indispensable in bringing about positive change. When workers bring complaints that cannot easily be categorized as sexual harassment or discrimination, representatives should be made aware that it could be caused by mobbing. If you are a unionized employee, make sure that you contact your representative and let them know what is going on. Specifically, union representatives can:

1. Investigate workplace mobbing.

2. Help establish conflict resolution/mediation teams to work with the employer on behalf of the individual employee experiencing a mobbing situation.

3. Make responses to mobbing a necessary part of the contract.

4. Lobby for changes to employment laws to include recourse for an unhealthy psychological environment including mobbing as another form of harassment.

STATE AND FEDERAL WORKFORCE AGENCIES ENFORCING LAWS

At the state level, the Labor Commissioner's task is to safeguard adherence to the labor laws and ensure job safety based on OSHA (Occupational Safety and Health Act) rules and regulations. The focus of OSHA laws has been the protection of the physical safety of employees. Workplace safety, however, requires also protection from emotional injury.

A person who has been mobbed, and as a consequence has suffered mental-mental injuries, a mental injury caused by mental trauma, can submit a complaint to the state Industrial Commissioner for investigation.

The State Civil Rights Commission investigates complaints based on discrimination under Title VII laws. When a complaint has substance but cannot be readily identified as discrimination, it might very well be a mobbing case. Consequently, the case may be referred to the state Industrial Commission.[12]

EDUCATORS—TEACHING RESPECTFUL CONDUCT AND CONFLICT RESOLUTION

Educators prepare the next generation of the workforce. In thousands of school districts across the U.S., educators in state agencies and private organizations have worked together over the past decades to bring conflict resolution skills into schools. Hundreds of thousands of students in the K-12 system have learned skills that help them deal with conflict constructively. They learn to deal with their anger to avert violence, to listen, to respect others' opinions, to adhere to a dialogue process, and to ask for help when they cannot work things out by themselves. They learn that there often are multiple truths. These are important skills essential in dealing with mobbing should they ever be involved in the dynamics of mobbing in their future workplaces. The U.S. is leading in these endeavors worldwide.[13]

Programs are also introduced in many schools that deal quite specifically with bullying behavior. Students are taught how to deal with bullies and how bullies can be helped to transform their behaviors. An example for such a program is the *No-Bullying Program* developed by Beverly Title and Lana D. Leonard from *Teaching Peace*.[14]

These endeavors must continue and be increased because they build an indispensable foundation for our youth to be better able to deal with conflicts at the workplace, at home, and in their communities, including those that occur in mobbing.

ORGANIZATIONAL CONSULTANTS AND TRAINERS—AT THE FOREFRONT

Nobody has quite as much insight into the core of an organization as organizational consultants. They can assume a great responsibility in spotting weak points in a structure that would allow for mobbing to occur. It is therefore of considerable importance that they understand the mobbing syndrome thoroughly and do not mistake it as a manifestation of simply difficult people.

And what about the role of trainers? In the context of mobbing, their work in alerting organizations to the syndrome and help in preventing it is crucial. They can carve out a whole new training field. These are some of the workshop, seminar and training topics that could be offered:

- How to Prevent Mobbing at the Workplace
- How to Deal with Mobbing
- Don't Succumb to Mobbing—Maintain Your Identity and Self-worth
- What Management Needs to Know about Mobbing
- Mobbing and the Law

LEGAL COMMUNITY—BEING BETTER PREPARED

Lawyers have a crucial role to play in the defense of mobbing victims. How many individuals come to them with a request for representation for a civil rights suit when, in fact, it is a mobbing case? How can they, based on the presently existing law, make a case for mobbing?

Legislators can begin to develop new laws or expand the existing laws to better deal with the reality of work abuse. Ideas the legal community may wish to consider:

1. Research how current laws can be interpreted to assist individuals subjected to mobbing in the workplace.

2. Assist in setting up a branch of legal aid, perhaps in cooperation with state job service and unemployment professionals to provide assistance with legal recourse to those victimized by mobbing, either with educational information involving recourse or with representation.

3. Make recommendations through the State Bar Associations to address mobbing issues, both with changes in existing laws and with reference material for attorneys representing employees victimized by mobbing.

4. Publish case stories in law journals.

5. Organize continuing education classes on the subject.

6. Invite victims of mobbing to speak at meetings and conferences.

7. Develop informational materials for state agencies such as the Labor or the Industrial Commissions.

As an example, we refer again to what occurred in Scandinavia as a result of increased awareness of mobbing. Sweden, Finland, and Norway now legally recognize the employee's right to both a physically and a mentally healthy work environment. The Swedish National Board of Occupational Safety and Health has approved three statutes to enforce this legislation, one of them especially regarding mobbing. One obligates the employer to internal control of the work environment on a regular basis in order to be able to take measures at an early stage. Another enforces direct interventions if mobbing occurs at the workplace. A third ordinance enforces the employer's responsibility for vocational rehabilitation once an employee has been on sick leave very often during one year or has been on sick leave for at least one month.[15]

In summary, it is our belief that the costs of mobbing must and can be considerably reduced with a concerted effort by all of us.

Chapter 9 Endnotes

1. Quoted with permission from a personal communication by Marie Lynette Hanthorn, November, 1998. M.L. Hanthorn is co-founder of Visibiliti, a communications and publishing company in Tuscon, AZ.

2. As quoted in C. Brady Wilson's article U.S. Businesses Suffer from Workplace Trauma. In:*Personnel Journal*, July 1991.

3. The Swedish Occupational Safety Ordinance, 1994.

4. In 1991 as much as approximately 25% of the work force above the age of 55 were retired early. Between 20% and 40% of the yearly number of early retirements was caused by poor psychosocial environments. Approximately every third to fifth early retiree in this age group had suffered from extensive mobbing. Quoted from Leymann's The Mobbing Encyclopedia; Bullying; Whistle-blowing. File 15100e on the Internet and based on personal discussions by Leymann with officials from the Swedish National Board of Social Insurance, 1993.

5. Leymann, 1998.

6. Quoted in Hoel et. al., 1999:204.

7. American Association of Suicidology, Washington, DC 20008, Tel. (202) 237-2280; <www.cyberpsych.org>.

8. It is almost impossible to accurately identify murder directly attributable to workplace issues from the federally available murder statistics as provided from the Department of Justice, Federal Bureau of Investigations, National Criminal Justice Reference Service, Tel. 304/625-5394.

9. See Loraleigh Keashly's article "Emotional Abuse in the Workplace: Conceptual and Empirical Issues" that summarizes the major research in the U.S. and Canada with respect to the definition and conceptualization of emotional abuse at the workplace. Keashly, 1998. See also Hoel et.al., 1999.

10. Quoted from Confidentiality Brochure, printed in the *EAP Association Exchange*, May/June 1996.

11. Wyatt and Hare, 1997:262.

12. The names of Industrial and Labor Commissions vary from state to state.

13. The Conflict Resolution in Education Network, CREnet, supports and advocates for the teaching and modeling of conflict resolution skills in every educational setting. For more information you may wish to contact: ACR (Association for Conflict Resolution, www.acresolution.org). 1527 New Hampshire Avenue, NW, Washington DC 20036, Tel. 202-667-9700, FAX 202-665-1968, <www.crenet.org>.

14. Title, Beverly, 1995.

15. Swedish National Board of Occupational Safety and Health, AFS, 1992; 1993:17; AFS 1994:1. These ordinances and statutes can be obtained at: Swedish National Board of Occupational Safety and Health, S-17184 Solna, Sweden. Publishing Services, Fax + 46-8-7309817.

◆ EPILOGUE ◆

Creating a Civilized
Work Culture

*Tacit rules of behavior exist to regulate interpersonal relations
and help define civility and fairness. Although the precise rules
vary across the spectrum of world communities, their function
is the same everywhere: They protect people in social encoun-
ters from damaging insults and personal harm.*

—Harvey Hornstein
Brutal Bosses and Their Prey

*The purpose of our existence is to help other human beings.
If we cannot do that, the least we can do is not to hurt them.*

—The Dalai Lama

◆

Taking a historic perspective, we must acknowledge that the culture
of work in Western Civilization, and in the U.S. specifically, has
developed in a phenomenal way. In the past 150 years, we have
moved from acceptance of slavery to laws that protect employees and
to companies that provide benefits.

Yet, today, this is not sufficient. The culture of work today also
means creating a nourishing environment.

In such a workplace, leaders empower, affirm and appreciate their co-workers. They encourage creativity, cooperation, team-work, trust, problem solving, open and honest communications, and conflict management. They provide employees with personal development opportunities and create an emotionally healthy and psychologically safe workplace. Employees, in such a workplace, participate in decision making, feel appreciated, and have a sense of belonging.

Companies that do just that do thrive. This is widely recognized, researched, and has been proven to be quite profitable.

This is without a doubt an important indication of how the work culture can become a reflection of a civil society, a society in which all people are valued and are treated with respect. All human beings are entitled to be treated in a respectful and helpful way to ensure their dignity. This is what is called civility. In such an environment mobbing is very unlikely to happen and if it does it will be stopped before it spreads. In such an environment individuals are not sacrificed for the greater good or for the greater good of only a few.

It is our belief that once mobbing awareness is raised, people will not be willing to accept demeaning behaviors as a normal part of any job. Employees will expect fair, just, and respectful treatment. Just as employees have come to expect benefit plans, a workplace respectful of diversity and free of sexual harassment, so they will demand a mobbing-free environment.

It is hoped that mobbing will be considered severe misconduct in the same way as assault, sexual harassment and discrimination, negligence, theft, and the sale and use of drugs have become a matter of the law to which individuals are held accountable.

Our exploration into workplace mobbing has also opened our own eyes to mobbing in other contexts as well. We believe that mobbing also happens in families, communities, in tightly knit organizations, and in politics. What is the difference in essence if a person is humiliated, ostracized, and forced out of a workplace to mobbing in these other contexts? Although circumstances are different, mobbing behaviors impact victims in a similarly destructive way as workplace mobbing, behaviors that produce great pain and distress, illness, misery, and social costs. Vigilance is required to safeguard human dignity, integrity, and creativity no matter what the context of human interactions is.

We hope that through awareness building, good education, and early warning, people who are caught up in the dynamics of mobbing—as perpetrators or as victims—will understand what is happening. Hopefully they will be able to acknowledge their own role in bringing about change.

If we can outlaw discrimination, we can also outlaw mobbing. Developing civility in the workplace will impact civility in society.

◆

BIBLIOGRAPHY

Adams, Andrea with Neil Crawford. 1992. *Bullying at Work: How to Confront and Overcome It*. London: Virago Press.

Amason, Allen C. and Hochwarter, Wayne A., et al. 1995. Conflict: An Important Dimension in Successful Management Teams. In: *Organizational Dynamics*. Autumn, 1995.

Atkins, Gary L. Behavioral Risk Management: A New Opportunity for EAP Growth and Development. In: *EAPA Exchange*, May/June 1997, vol.27, no. 3, p. 15.

Autry, James A. 1992. *Love and Profit. The Art of Caring Leadership*. New York: Avon Books.

Bassman, Emily S. 1992. *Abuse in the Workplace; Management Remedies and Bottom Line Impact*. Westport, Connecticut: Quorum Book.

Baumeister, Roy F., Smart, Laura; Boden, Joseph M.; 1996. Relation of Threatened Egotism to Violence and Agression: The Dark Side of High Self-Esteem. In: *Psychological Review*, 1996, Vol. 103, No. 1, 5-33.

Bennett, Mark W.; Polden, Donald J; Rubin, Howard J. 1998. *Employment Relationships; Law and Practice*. New York, Aspen Law & Business.

Beasley, John; Rayner, Charlottte. 1997. Bullying at Work. After Andrea Adams. In: *Journal of Community & Applied Social Psychology*, Vol. 7, 177-180 (1997).

Brodsky, Carroll M. 1976. *The Harassed Worker*. Lexington, MA: D.C. Heath and Company.

Burns, David D. 1990. *The Feeling Good Handbook*. New York: A Plume Book/Penguins Books.

Butler, Gillian; Hope, Tony. 1995. *Managing Your Mind. The Mental Fitness Guide*. New York: Oxford University Press.

Chappell, Duncan; Di Martino, Vittorio. 1998. *Violence at Work*, Geneva: International Labour Office.

Cliff, Hakim. 1994. *We Are All Self-Employed. The New Social Contract for Working in a Changing World*. San Francisco: Berrett-Koehler Publishers, Inc.

Cortina, Lilia M. et al. 2001. Incivility in the Workplace: Incidence and Impact. *Journal of Occupational Health Psychology*. Vol. 6, No. 1, 64-80.

Cousins, Norman. 1979. *Anatomy of an Illness as Perceived by the Patient*. New York: W. W. Norton & Company.

Covey, Stephen R. 1989. *The Seven Habits of Highly Effective People. Powerful Lessons on Personal Change*. New York: Fireside.

Denenberg, Richard V., Braverman, Mark. 1999. *The Violence-Prone Workplace: A New Approach to Dealing with Hostile, Threatening, and Uncivil Behavior*. Cornell University Press.

Einarsen, Ståle; Rakens, Bjorn Inge. 1997. Harassment in the Workplace and the Victimization of Men. In: *Violence and Victims*, Vol. 12, No.3, 247-263.

Field, Tim. 1996. *Bully in Sight. How to Predict, Resist, Challenge and Combat Workplace Bullying. Overcoming the Silence and Denial by which Abuse Thrives*. Oxfordshire: Success Unlimited.

Golden, Thomas R. 1996. *Swallowed by a Snake: The Gift of the Masculine Side of Healing*. Gaithersburg, MD: Golden Healing Publishing LLC.

Goleman, Daniel. 1995. *Emotional Intelligence*. New York: Bantam Books.

Goleman, Daniel. 1998. *Working with Emotional Intelligence*. New York: Bantam Books.

Gray, John, 1992. *Men Are from Mars, Women Are from Venus*. New York: HarperCollins Publishers.

Grund, Uwe. 1995. Wenn die Hemmschwellen sinken. Die Aufgabe der Gewerkschaften: Aufklaerung und Praevention. In: Leymann, Heinz (Ed.). *Der neue Mobbing Bericht. Erfahrungen und Initiativen, Auswege und Hilfsangebote*. Hamburg: RowohltTaschenbuch Verlag GmbH.

Hall, Francine, S. 1991. Dysfunctional Managers. The Next Human Resource Challenge. In: *Organizational Dynamics*. Autumn, 1991.

Hirigoyen, Marie France. 2000. *Stalking the Soul. Emotional Abuse and the Erosion of Identity*. New York, Helen Marx Books.

Hoel, Helge; Rayner, Charlotte; Cooper, Cary L. 1999. Workplace Bullying. In: *International Review of Industrial and Organizational Psychology*. Vol. 14, p. 195-230.

Hornstein, Harvey A. 1996. *Brutal Bosses and their Prey. How to Identify and Overcome Abuse in the Workplace*. New York: Riverhead Books.

Keashly, Loraleigh. 1998. Emotional Abuse in the Workplace: Conceptual and Empirical Issues. In: *Journal of Emotional Abuse*, Vol. 1 (1) 1998, p. 85-117.

Laabs, Jennifer J. 1992. HR's Vital Role at Levi Strauss. In: *Personnel Journal*, December, 1992, Vol.71, No.12.

Leymann, Heinz. 1990. Mobbing and Psychological Terror at Workplaces. In: *Violence and Victims*. Vol. 5, No. 2.

Leymann, Heinz. 1993. *Mobbing. Psychoterror am Arbeitsplatz und wie man sich dagegen wehren kann*. Hamburg: Rowohlt Taschenbuch Verlag GmbH.

Leymann, Heinz (Ed.). 1995. *Der neue Mobbing Bericht. Erfahrungen und Initiativen, Auswege und Hilfsangebote*. Hamburg: Rowohlt Taschenbuch Verlag GmbH.

Leymann, Heinz. 1996. The Content and Development of Mobbing at Work. In: *European Journal of Work and Organizational Psychology, 5 (2)*.

Leymann, Heinz, and Gustafsson, Anneli. 1996. Mobbing at Work and the Development of Post-traumatic Stress Disorders. In: *European Journal of Work and Organizational Psychology., 5 (2)*.

Leymann, Heinz. 1997. *The Mobbing Encyclopaedia*. Internet Resource.

Leymann, Heinz, and Gustafsson, Annelie, 1998. Suicides Due to Mobbing/Bullying—About Nurses' High Risks in the Labour Market. Geneva: WHO (World Health Organization) Internal Report. (The Swedish original is published by Nordstedts Juridiska in Stockholm, 1998.)

Lorenz, Konrad, 1963. *Das sogennante Boese*. Wien: Dr. G. Borotha-Schoeler Verlag.

Lorenz, Konrad, 1991. *Here am I - Where are You? The Behavior of the Greylag Goose*. New York: Harcourt Brace Jovanovich.

Maccoby, Michael. 2000. Narcissistic Leaders: The Incredible Pros, the Inevitable Cons. *Harvard Business Review*, Vol. 78, Number 1, 68-77.

Mahoney, Stanley C. 1967. *The Art of Helping People Effectively*. New York: Association Press.

Marais, Susan and Herman, Magriet. 1997. *Corporate Hyenas at Work! How to Spot and Outwirt Them by Being Hyenawise*. Pretoria: Kagiso Publishers.

Moats Kennedy, Marilyn. 1985. *Office Warfare. Strategies for Getting Ahead in the Aggressive '80's.* New York: MacMillan Publishing Company.

Namie, Gary and Namie, Ruth. 2000. *The Bully at Work. What You Can Do to Stop the Hurt and Reclaim Your Dignity on the Job.* Naperville, IL: Sourcebooks, Inc.

Niedl, Klaus. 1995. *Mobbing/Bullying am Arbeitsplatz. Eine empirische Analyse zum Phaenomen sowie zu personalwirtschaftlich relevanten Effekten von systematischen Feindseligkeiten.* Muenchen und Mering: Rainer Hampp Verlag.

Neuman, Joel H. and Baron, Robert A. 1997. Aggression in the Workplace. In: R.A. GiacaPone and J. Greengerg (Eds.). *Antisocial Behaviors in Organizations.* Thousand Oaks, CA: Sage.

Peck, M. Scott. 1998. *People of the Lie. The Hope for Healing Human Evil.* New York: Touchstone.

Price Spratlen, Lois. 1995. Interpersonal Conflict Which Includes Mistreatment in a University Workplace. In: *Violence and Victims,* Vol. 10, No.4, 1995, 285-297.

Randall, Peter. 1997. *Adult Bullying. Perpetrators and Victims.* New York: Routledge.

Rayner, Charlotte. 1997. The Incidence of Workplace Bullying. In: *Journal of Community & Applied Social Psychology,* Vol. 7, 199-208.

Rayner, Charlotte; Hoel, Helge. 1997. A Summary Review of Literature Relating to Workplace Bullying. In: *Journal of Community & Applied Social Psychology,* Vol. 7, 181-191.

Rayner, Charlotte; Hoel, Helge, and Cooper, Cary L. 2001. *Workplace Bullying: What We Know, Who Is to Blame, and What Can We Do?* London: Taylor & Francis.

Ryan, Kathleen D. and Oestreich, Daniel K. 1991. *Driving Fear out of the Workplace. How to Overcome the Invisible Barriers to Quality, Productivity, and Innovation.* San Francisco: Jossey-Bass Publishers.

Sack, Steven Mitchell. 1998. *The Working Woman's Legal Survival Guide.* Paramus, NJ: Prentice Hall Press.

Schulze, Sigrid. 1996. *Konfliktzone Buero. Der Anti-Mobbing-Ratgeber.* Muenchen: Humboldt-Taschenbuchverlag.

Schultz, Vicki. 1998. Reconceptualizing Sexual Harassment. *The Yale Law Journal*, Vol. 107, Number 6, April 1998.

Schuepbach, Karin and Torre, Rossella. 1996. *Mobbing. Verstehen - Ueberwinden -Vermeiden. Ein Leitfaden fuer Fuehrungskraefte und Personalverantwortliche*. Zuerich: Kaufmaennischer Verband.

Tannen, Deborah. 1990. *You Just Don't Understand*. New York: William Morrow and Company, Inc.

Title, Beverly and Leonard, Lana S. Teaching Peace. *The No-Bullying Program*. P.O. Box. 412, Hygiene, Co, 80533. Internet: <info@teachingpeace.org>.

Title, Beverly B. 1995. *Bully-Victim Conflict. An Overview for Educators*. Published by Johnson Institute, Minneapolis.

Victimization at Work. 1994. *Statute Book of the Swedish National Board of Occupational Safety and Health*. Ordinance Swedish National Board of Occupational Safety and Health. Solna, Sweden.

Waniorek, Linda and Axel. 1994. Mobbing: *Wenn der Arbeitsplatz zur Hoelle wird*. Muenchen: mvg verlag.

Westhues, Kenneth. 1998. *Eliminating Professors. A Guide to the Dismissal Process*. Queenston, Canada: Kempner Collegium Publications.

Westhues, Kenneth. 2002 (forthcoming). *Human Sacrifice in Universities: Toronto versus Richardson* (proposed title). Lewiston, New York: Kempner Collegium Publications.

Wilson, Brady, C. 1991. U.S. Businesses Suffer from Workplace Trauma. In: *Personnel Journal*. July, p. 47-50.

Wyatt, Judith and Hare, Chauncey. 1997. *Work Abuse. How to Recognize and Survive It*. Rochester, Vermont: Schenkman Books, Inc.

Yamada, David C. 2000. The Phenomenon of "Workplace Bullying" and the Need for Status-Blind Hostile Work Environment Protection. *The Georgetown Law Journal*, Vol. 88, Number 3, 475-536.

Zapf, Dieter and Leymann, Heinz, Eds. 1996. Mobbing and Victimization at Work. *European Journal of Work and Organizational Psychology*. Vol. 5, Number 2.

INDEX

ACKNOWLEDGEMENTS

We owe a debt of gratitude to our interview partners for participating in this project. Their stories are the material on which this book is based and their words are the illustrations that make our points real. We thank them for giving their time and their insights.

Our deepest thanks to our families and friends for reading early versions of our writing, for their support, their advice and for their faith in us. We thank Aaron L. Davenport, Stephanie Davenport, Ursula Schoeni, Janet S. Karon, Clyde Schwartz, Melissa Schwartz, Satuila and Helm Stierlin, James and Jean Vammen.

We are especially indebted to Mark Bennett, Bernie Kemp, Paul Lambakis, Daniel Maguire and David Yamada, for critically reading selected chapters or the entire draft and for helping us to refine our thinking.

We thank Carroll Brodsky, Dennis Brown, Dan Clark, Marie L. Hanthorn, Steven L. Howard, Loraleigh Keashly, Kathy Myers, Nicole Rafter, Charlotte Rayner, Kathy Skinner, Tim Taylor, and Kenneth Westhues, for their approval, cheers, helpful comments, and for pointing out literature and sending current research.

And we wish to thank the circle of expert advisers who helped provide information: Don Grove, former Executive Director, Iowa Civil Rights Commission; Jon E. Heitland, Chief Deputy, Workers' Compensation Commissioner, Iowa Workforce Development; Michael R. Hoffmann, PLC Attorney, Workers' Compensation; Nathenia Johnson, People Systems Consultant, Saturn Corporation; Byron K. Orton, Iowa Labor Commissioner; Alfredo Parrish, Trial Attorney; Iris J. Post, Workers' Compensation Commissioner, Iowa Workforce Development; Robin Winburn, Human Resources Department, Policy Planner, Levi Strauss & Co.

We thank the Saturn Corporation for permission to quote their philosophy and conflict resolution procedures, and Levi Strauss & Co. for permission to quote portions from their mission and aspiration statements.

Heinz Leymann read our first draft and gave us substantive advice and unfaltering encouragement. We corresponded for a year and met with him in November 1998. Shortly before his death in January 1999, we received his foreword for this book. We are forever grateful for his support.

AUTHORS AND ILLUSTRATOR

Noa Davenport, Ph.D., of Swiss origin, is a teacher with an academic background in cultural anthropology. She has worked internationally in research and administration, in governmental and nonprofit organizations, in higher education and business. She is an adjunct assistant professor at Iowa State University, and a member of the Faculty at William Penn University, College for Working Adults, Iowa. She is principal of DNZ Training and Consulting working internationally with a focus on conflict resolution education at the workplace, in schools, and in communities. More information about workshops and consulting is available at *www.dnztraininginternational.com.*

Ruth Distler Schwartz, M.S., has spent most of her career in management in nonprofit organizations, higher education and healthcare. In addition to managing organizations of 5 to 400 employees, she has designed executive and professional development programs including a distinguished scholars program and a social issues series. She is the editor of "Know Your Rights: Understanding What You Must Do If You Are Ever a Suspect in a Criminal Case." President of R. A. Schwartz & Associates, a national management consulting firm, she now lives in Des Moines, Iowa. More information is available at *www.raschwartz.com.*

Gail Pursell Elliott, a speaker, author, educator, human resources and training consultant, is founder of Innovations "Training With A Can-Do Attitude"TM promoting Dignity and Respect, No Exceptions, in companies and communities nationwide. First published in 1970, she is a Mensan who is the author of business, motivational, inspirational articles and poetry as well as the weekly column "Food For Thought." In addition to her contracted work, Gail presents sessions on Dignity and Respect and Mobbing Awareness for students as a donated service. Her website is *www.innovations-training.com.*

Sabra Bruna Vidali was born in Switzerland. She grew up in the United States and graduated from art school in Florence, Italy. She lives partially in Italy and partially in Indiana and works as a freelance illustrator, webpage designer, and translator. Her webpage is *www.textweaver.com*.

The authors are available for trainings or to speak at conferences and meetings. Please call or write to:

◆ Noa Davenport: Tel. 641-385-2216;
   email: info@dnztraininginternational.com
◆ Ruth Distler Schwartz: Tel. 515-255-4536;
   email: rasch@dmreg.infi.net
◆ Gail Pursell Elliott: 515-231-8828;
   email: info@innovations-training.com

For more information about MOBBING, Emotional Abuse in the American Workplace, or to link to the authors' websites, please see: *www.mobbing-usa.com*.